Guide to the
GOLDEN GATE
National Recreation Area

Dorothy L. Whitnah

Wilderness Press
BERKELEY

Photography (except historical photos) and design by L. Linkhart

Produced in cooperation with the National Park Service

Acknowledgments

Thanks are due to the following persons, who have provided companionship, food, information, miscellaneous supplies and moral support: Robert Bardell, D. Steven Corey, Richard H. Dillon, John R. Turner Ettlinger, Franklin Gilliam, Stephen G. Herrick, Cecelia Hurwich, Serena Jutkovitz, Alfred L. Kennedy, Emery and Noelle Liebrenz, Luther and Virginia Linkhart, Kent McCarthy, Stephanie McGowan, Amy Meyer, Emily Ross, Carol Sarkis, Jeff Schaffer, Ann and Gregory Whipple, Caroline, Jason, Lucille and Thomas Winnett, and Steve Heath and John Sage of the GGNRA staff.

Published by Wilderness Press, 2440 Bancroft Way, Berkeley, CA 94704

TABLE OF CONTENTS

INTRODUCTION

"In order to preserve for public use and enjoyment certain areas of Marin and San Francisco Counties, California, possessing outstanding natural, historic, scenic, and recreational values, and in order to provide for the maintenance of needed recreational open space necessary to urban environment and planning, the Golden Gate National Recreation Area is hereby established. In the management of the recreation area, the Secretary of the Interior . . . shall utilize the resources in a manner which will provide for recreation and educational opportunities consistent with sound principles of land use planning and management. In carrying out the provisions of this Act, the Secretary shall preserve the recreation area, as far as possible, in its natural setting, and protect it from development and uses which would destroy the scenic beauty and natural character of the area."
—PUBLIC LAW 92-589

L ast year as I was driving a visiting Englishman across the Golden Gate Bridge he remarked, "I can't understand why San Franciscans are so defensive about their City. True, the museums aren't up to Los Angeles's standards, and the symphony and the opera may not be quite as good as New York's or Chicago's—but for climate and physical beauty no other city in the U. S. can even come close to it!"

Many Bay Areans don't yet realize that their home is the scene of an unprecedented experiment in parks, the Golden Gate National Recreation Area. What makes the GGNRA unique?

First, the GGNRA and neighboring Point Reyes National Seashore together contain over 100,000 acres—the largest

◁ *Two young adventurers chase the surf on a wild and windy day at Tennessee Cove* national park adjoining a major metropolitan center in the world. Another unusual feature of the GGNRA is the prominent role that ordinary citizens have played, first in establishing it and then in planning for its future. A grassroots organization called People for a Golden Gate National Recreation Area (pronounced "piff-ganura"), led by dedicated volunteer co-chairmen Dr. Edgar Wayburn and Amy Meyer, was formed in 1971 to lobby for the park's creation. The Congressional move to establish the GGNRA was bipartisan from its beginning in 1972. Democrat Phillip Burton and Republican William Mailliard sponsored the legislation in the House, Democrats Alan Cranston and John Tunney in the Senate, and it moved through Congress with amazing ease. (That 1972 was an election year may not have hurt it.) On October 27, 1972, President Nixon signed the bill bringing the park into existence.

The act that established the GGNRA also mandated the creation of a Citizen's Advisory Commission to oversee its development and that of neighboring Point Reyes National Seashore and to keep the National Park Service informed of the people's wishes and hopes for the two parks. The 15-member Commission now contains, in addition to the tireless Dr. Wayburn and Mrs. Meyer, representatives from a variety of economic and ethnic groups in San Francisco, Marin and the East Bay. The Commission meets regularly at various spots in Marin and San Francisco counties, and these meetings are *open to the public.* They are, in fact, a fascinating example of democracy in action at the town-meeting level, as concerned citizens rise to present their views on issues ranging from the installation of tennis courts on one of Fort Mason's piers to the transfer of Mount Tamalpais from the state to the national park system.

The National Park Service has gone out of its way from the beginning to seek public participation in planning the GGNRA, even beyond that provided by the Citizens' Advisory Commission. For one reason, they want this to be a unique model for a large park located in a heterogeneous metropolitan area—an example that can be followed all over the world for decades to come. For another reason, a park of the size, complexity and diversity of combined GGNRA/Point Reyes (not

Many of the trails in the GGNRA are old ranch roads

Historic tug and steam schooner at the Hyde Street Pier

World War II barracks being removed from Fort Baker after 30 years of service

to mention the contiguous public recreational land owned by the state, counties, cities, water districts and the military) presents a mind-boggling array of possibilities. To take just one example—buildings—the PFGGNRA's *Greenbelt Gazette* points out: "In a park that includes 1600 barns, bunkers, homes, farmhouses, barracks and warehouses, the structure best suited for a particular purpose can be selected." Finally, the NPS is determined not to risk any repetition of the public-relations debacle it went through in Yosemite, where the concessionaire, Music Corporation of America, made the front pages of the nation when it was revealed to be encouraging large conventions in the valley and painting boulders white for a commercial television series.

During 1975 and 1976 the NPS held nearly 200 public workshop among as wide as possible a variety of groups in the Bay Area—from the Albany Lions Club to the Japanese Center Youth Council to the Booker T. Washington Community Center. The purpose was to find out what a cross-section of the public, including senior citizens and inner-city residents as well as middle-class conservation activists, really wanted and needed from the GGNRA and Point Reyes. It is perhaps a hopeful augury for the future of our national parks that the GGNRA's first Superintendent, the able William J. Whalen, under whose leadership these workshops were held, was subsequently appointed head of the NPS—the youngest man ever to hold the post.

The preliminary result of the workshop meetings emerged in 1977 as a 500-page summary entitled *Assessment of Alternatives for the General Management Plan for the Golden Gate National Recreation Area and Point Reyes National Seashore*, which can be studied at libraries and NPS offices. A condensed version entitled *A People's Guide to the Future of the National Parks Next Door* is available *free* from headquarters. This is must reading for everyone who is concerned with the Bay

Should Sutro Baths be restored?

Area's open-space and recreational scene, or with the political, economic and sociological considerations involved in park planning. To get a copy, phone 556-2920 or 556-0560; or write the GGNRA, Fort Mason, San Francisco, CA 94123.

The workshop participants were in general agreement that the northern sections should be left in a relatively primitive and rural state, while most new facilities and activities should be located in the southern sections, which are already the most developed. As a park spokesman put it, "What's attractive about the parks is what's already there. Our job is really to polish the jewels, not to create new attractions."

The published *Assessment* study has boiled workshop participants' and other park visitors' suggestions down to four alternatives for most of the areas:

A—Keep the park as is: The park should maintain things as they are with few increases in management, programs or facilities.

B—Maximize natural qualities: Planning actions should increase the contrast between the city and the park by maximizing open space, minimizing facilities, and restoring natural landscapes.

C—Create a place for discovery: The park should be a "laboratory for learning," providing necessary programs and facilities to encourage visitors' understanding of historic, cultural, and natural resources.

D—Provide places for enjoyment: The park is a valuable addition to Bay Area open space and should provide many opportunities for leisure-time activities, emphasizing cultural and recreational programs.

The report estimates the cost of each alternative. It also considers such vital matters as transportation to and in the parks, visitor services and overnight use. The NPS will continue to seek out public opinion on the various alternatives before making final decisions. Let them know what you think!

Walking alone on the edge of the continent

NATURAL AND SCENIC VALUES

The GGNRA includes just about every kind of plant-and-animal community to be found in northern California: beaches, marshlands, ocean cliffs, meadows, rolling hills, and forests of redwood, Douglas fir, and oak and madrone. Each of these ecosystems contains the plant and animal life natural to it, and in addition many bird species from other parts of the world visit the area seasonally.

The scenery includes the world-famous vistas of the Golden Gate as viewed from the San Francisco and Marin headlands and from the islands in the Bay; the rugged Marin seacoast; and forested Bolinas Ridge. Adjoining the GGNRA are Mt. Tamalpais and Muir Woods, also in the public domain. Together, all these natural wonders form an unparalleled magnet attracting

Geology class examining the rock formation at the east end of Bakers Beach

residents and tourists to sightsee, photograph and just wander around.

Another of the area's world-famous natural wonders—although perhaps not properly labeled an attraction, except to geologists—is the San Andreas fault zone, which runs along the boundary between the GGNRA and Point Reyes National Seashore.

Most geologists now accept the idea that the outer layer of the earth is composed of huge, contiguous crustal plates, about 60 miles thick. These plates are gliding over a hot, molten layer 200 miles thick. In some places, two plates meet head-on, and one overrides the other. In other places, two plates glide laterally past each other. That's what's happening in the San Andreas fault zone, which is the interface between the Pacific plate to the west and the North American plate to the east. At present the Pacific plate is moving northwest relative to the North American plate at a rate of slightly more than 2 inches a year —although during the earthquake of 1906 it moved as much as 20 feet in a few minutes. Point Reyes is on the Pacific plate, and is formed of entirely different, granitic rock than the area to the east of it.

Most of the GGNRA consists of rocks of a melange called the Franciscan Formation. The main constituents of this formation are sedimentary rocks—graywacke, shale, chert and a small amount of limestone—that were thoroughly crumpled and jumbled by the pressure of the two plates against each other. The Franciscan Formation also includes some metamorphic rocks, mainly blue and green schists, and some "pillow" basalt resulting from eruptions of lava upon the sea floor. Later, some igneous rock—peridotite—was injected into the Franciscan Formation, and the heat of this injection converted some peridotite to serpentine. Serpentine is conspicuous in several parts of the GGNRA and adjoining areas.

Until the development of plate-tectonic theory, geologists were hard put to explain the bewildering jumble of the Franciscan Formation: it seemed that to produce some of these minerals and rocks in such scrambled condition would have required pressures of an order found not less than 50,000 feet below the earth's surface. Now it appears that much of the necessary pressure was lateral, rather than vertical.

HISTORIC VALUES

The area now occupied by the GGNRA has played a crucial role in California's history. Indeed, it is largely for that reason that much of this land remained in the public domain. The feature that has given the GGNRA its great scenic values—namely, its position on each side of the only entrance to San Francisco Bay—obviously has given it great strategic value also.

Inside Fort Point looking up at the substructure of the Golden Gate Bridge

The military of three successive governments (those of Spain, Mexico and the U.S.) have occupied and fortified the headlands on both sides of the Golden Gate, and the islands in the Bay, since the San Francisco Presidio was established in 1776. If it had not been for the presence of the military, no doubt most of this land would long ago have been bought up by private developers and converted into housing tracts. It is only within the past decade, when the Defense Department has come to rely on long-range missile systems located far from urban areas, that the Golden Gate has ceased to be of strategic importance. Fortunately, the environmental movement peaked about this time, so much of this land has been transferred from the Army to the NPS. Plenty of fortifications remain, however. In fact, one of the most fascinating aspects of the GGNRA is that it provides a sort of inadvertent museum of changing military technology over two centuries.

The GGNRA includes a number of historic civilian sites, too. Among the best-known are the Cliff House and the remains of Sutro Baths.

Here is a brief chronology of events that have left their mark on the land now occupied by the GGNRA, Point Reyes National Seashore and neighboring parks:

10,000? B.C.-ca. 1800 A.D.—Coast Miwok Indians inhabit Marin County, Costanoan Indians the San Francisco peninsula.

1579—Francis Drake careens his ship, the *Golden Hind*, somewhere in northern California (probably Drakes Bay) and claims the land for Queen Elizabeth I.

1769—Gaspar de Portola commands an overland expedition from Baja California north to San Diego and subsequently to Monterey and the San Francisco Peninsula; a scouting expedition under Jose Ortega discovers San Francisco Bay.

Site of the old Spanish gun battery at Fort Mason that once guarded the entrance to San Francisco Bay

Father Junipero Serra founds the first California mission, San Diego de Alcala.

1775—Juan Manuel de Ayala brings the *San Carlos* into San Francisco Bay and surveys it.

1775-76—Juan Bautista de Anza leads a party of colonists overland from Sonora, Mexico, to San Francisco Bay.

1776—Jose Joaquin Moraga establishes the Presidio of San Francisco; Father Francisco Palou dedicates Mission San Francisco de Asis (now generally called Mission Dolores).

1812—Russians establish a post at Fort Ross for hunting, ranching and trading.

1817—Mission San Rafael Arcangel is founded.

1825—California officially becomes a

Cannon with cannoneer and plenty of ammunition on Alcatraz Island during the 1860's
(PHOTO, COURTESY GGNRA)

province of the new Republic of Mexico.

1833—The Mexican government orders the secularization of the California missions.

1841—The Russians leave Fort Ross. The first group of American overland immigrants reaches California.

1846—War breaks out between the United States and Mexico. American settlers in Sonoma proclaim California the "Bear Flag Republic." Commodore John D. Sloat raises the American flag at Monterey and declares California annexed to the United States.

1847—After a few skirmishes with the Mexicans, United States forces take over all of California.

1848—James Marshall discovers gold on the American River. The Mexican

War is concluded by the Treaty of Guadalupe Hidalgo, which cedes California to the United States.

1849—Argonauts come from all parts of the world to take part in the Gold Rush; San Francisco becomes an instant cosmopolis.

1850—California is admitted to the Union.

1850 on—The Army fortifies the San Francisco and Marin headlands and Alcatraz and Angel islands.

1861-64—During the Civil War, California remains loyal to the Union.

1869—The Central Pacific and the Union Pacific join tracks at Promontory Point, Utah, connecting California by rail to the eastern United States.

1892—John Muir and friends found the Sierra Club.

Adolph Sutro's magnificent gingerbread Cliff House (1896-1907) and Seal Rocks from Sutro Heights (W.C. BILLINGTON PHOTOGRAPH, COURTESY OF MARILYN BLAISDELL COLLECTION)

1902—The first California state park is established, at Big Basin in Santa Cruz County.

1906—Earthquake and fire destroy most of San Francisco.

1908—Muir Woods becomes a national monument.

1912—The Tamalpais Conservation Club is founded.

1915—The Panama Pacific International Exposition in what is now San Francisco's Marina District celebrates the construction of the Panama Canal and the reconstruction of San Francisco.

1928—Mt. Tamalpais becomes a state park.

1937—The Golden Gate Bridge opens.

1941-45—World War II draws thousands of workers to the Bay Area's industries, particularly its shipyards.

1945 on—California experiences unprecedented population growth and consequent urbanization.

1962—Congress authorizes Point Reyes National Seashore.

1972—Congress authorizes the GGRNA. California voters approve an initiative establishing a commission to regulate all coastal development.

GETTING TO THE PARKS

The *Assessments* publication points out the disquieting fact that 99 per cent of the visitors to the Marin sections of the parks drive there. And no doubt if the GGNRA had been set up 10 years earlier, its planners would have unquestioningly oriented it to the private automobile, arranging for more and wider access roads, more and bigger parking lots, extensive trailer parks and large car-camping areas. By the mid-1970's, however, both the NPS and much of the public had begun to fight back against the tyranny of the automobile—especially in the Bay Area, which spawned the first anti-freeway revolt in the country.

The public workshops sponsored by the NPS devoted considerable attention to questions of transportation. Areas that are not served by public transit are, in effect, off-limits to a large number of the citizenry—the very old, the very young, the very poor, the physically handicapped, and ethnic minorities—just the groups the NPS is trying to attract to these parks. Furthermore, extensive reliance on the private auto produces noise and air pollution in the parks and traffic congestion on the access roads and in the small communities adjacent to the parks, such as Stinson Beach and Olema. And, of course, we are finally becoming aware that the private automobile is one of the most inefficient, expensive and resource-wasteful methods of moving large numbers of people short distances that has ever been devised.

The NPS workshops came up with a number of suggestions for future alternatives to the automobile—e.g., regular shuttle buses from Fort Mason to Marin County; extensive ferry service all around the Bay; and the revival of the Belt Line railroad around the San Francisco waterfront. Of course, all these proposals cost money, and some of them require cooperation between rival bureaucracies. Meanwhile, we must make do with what public transit already exists. It is provided by the Golden Gate Bridge, Highway and Transportation District (GGT), the San Francisco Municipal Railway (Muni) and a few ferry lines.

GGT, which operates in San Fran-

A pollution-free way to get from San Francisco to Marin County

Golden Gate Transit runs buses every weekend to Pan Toll on Mt. Tamalpais

cisco, Marin and Sonoma counties, has promoted remarkably innovative programs designed to lure drivers out of their cars. Once in a while GGT backslides: for a few weeks in 1976 they cancelled the hikers' special weekend buses over Panoramic Highway on Mt. Tamalpais, until public outcry caused them to reinstitute the service, with small buses that can cope with the narrow, twisting roads. On the whole, however, GGT is years ahead of most other transit systems. Its buses are comfortable and convenient, and their schedules are updated regularly. At this point it remains to be seen whether GGT's ferry system—which has been plagued by almost as many cost overruns, delays in delivery, equipment failures and operational accidents as Bay Area Rapid Transit—represents the wave of the future or just an expensive voyage into nostalgia; if the latter, at least it's a pleasant voyage. Cynics and car commuters point out, correctly, that

GGT can afford these adventures in public transit only because it siphons off to them money from the auto tolls it continues to levy, and occasionally raise, on the Golden Gate Bridge. If gas gets scarcer and more expensive, however, the GGT directors may prove to have been wise before their time.

For information about routes and schedules, phone: from San Francisco, 332-6600; from Marin County, 453-2100; from Sonoma County, 544-1323. You can pick up printed schedules from GGT headquarters at the Golden Gate Bridge toll plaza.

San Francisco's Muni suffers the woes common to U.S. urban public transit systems in the 1970s: deteriorating, undermaintained vehicles, vandalism and occasional violence. Still, it's certainly more convenient than driving a car to a crowded place like Aquatic Park. (This statement does not apply to the Muni's cable cars, however, for which one usually has to

Point Diablo and the City from Battery Rathbone-McIndoe during one of Marin County's rare snowfalls

Unfortunately, most poison oak is not as well identified as this stand in Samuel P. Taylor Park

Visitors to the GGNRA should respect the warning signs posted by the Park Service

wait in line for at least half an hour.)

For information on routes and schedules, phone 673-MUNI. Printed schedules and an extremely helpful leaflet called "Ride the Muni," which maps all the routes, are available from the San Francisco Municipal Railway, 949 Presidio Avenue, San Francisco 94115, and from the Redwood Empire Association, 476 Post Street, San Francisco 94102.

The ferries to Alcatraz and Angel islands are discussed in their respective chapters.

A FEW THINGS TO REMEMBER

Motorized vehicles are restricted to paved roads; they are not allowed on trails or in the backcountry.

Dogs must be on leash, except in a few beach areas where they are specifically permitted to run free. Dogs are not allowed on many of the trails.

Don't light fires except in the park's grills and fire rings; don't smoke on the trails.

Don't bring firearms into the park:

hunting is not permitted in the GGNRA.

Take a water canteen on any extended outing: the surface water in much of the GGNRA is polluted.

Obey warning signs about the dangers of swimming, climbing on cliffs and exploring old bunkers. The Park Service has posted these signs for good reasons.

The GGNRA contains one dangerous animal, the western rattlesnake, and one dangerous plant, poison oak. The rattlesnake is rarely encountered, but poison oak is found on many of the trails in Marin County. It is shiny green in spring, brilliant red in late summer and fall.

Don't leave any litter behind.

Don't molest any animal or remove any plant.

MAPS: C.E. Erickson & Associates have issued a map of the GGNRA similar in format to their trail maps of Mt. Tamalpais and Point Reyes; it is available at many book and map stores.

The GGNRA has issued a trail guide to Marin Headlands, available at the ranger stations for $.25.

The most detailed maps, and the most fun for map-lovers to study, are those issued by the U.S. Geological Survey in its 7.5-minute topographic series (scale 1:24,000, or 1 inch = 2000 feet). They are available in map stores and at the local USGS office at 555 Battery Street, San Francisco. The ones that cover the GGNRA are: San Francisco South, San Francisco North, Point Bonita, Bolinas, San Rafael, Inverness and San Geronimo. Another useful USGS map is that of Point Reyes National Seashore and Vicinity (scale 1:48,000) issued in 1973.

AREA CODE: All the phone numbers in this book are in area code 415.

RECOMMENDED READING

DOSS, MARGOT PATTERSON, *Paths of Gold: In and Around the Golden Gate National Recreation Area.* San Francisco: Chronicle Books, 1974.

—, *San Francisco at Your Feet.* Rev. ed. New York: Grove Press, 1974.

GEBHARD, DAVID, *et al., A Guide to Architecture in San Francisco and Northern California.* 2nd ed. Santa Barbara and Salt Lake City: Peregrine Smith, 1976.

GILLIAM, HAROLD, and MICHAEL BRY, *The Natural World of San Francisco.* Garden City, New York: Doubleday, 1967.

GILLIAM, HAROLD, *San Francisco Bay.* Garden City, New York: Doubleday, 1957.

—, *The San Francisco Experience.* Garden City, New York: Doubleday, 1972.

GUDDE, ERWIN G. *California Place Names.* 3rd ed. Berkeley, Los Angeles and London: University of California Press, 1969.

HANSEN, GLADYS, ed., *San Francisco: The Bay and Its Cities.* Rev. ed. New York: Hastings House, 1973. American Guide Series.

HOOVER, MILDRED B., *et al., Historic Spots in California.* 3rd ed. Stanford, Stanford University Press, 1966.

LEWIS, OSCAR, *San Francisco: Mission to Metropolis.* Berkeley: Howell-North, 1966.

MARIN COUNTY AMERICAN REVOLUTION BICENTENNIAL COMMISSION, *Old Marin with Love.* 1976.

MASON, JACK, and HELEN VAN CLEAVE PARK, *Early Marin.* 2nd rev. ed. Inverness: North Shore Books, 1976.

MASON, JACK, and THOMAS J. BARFIELD, *Last Stage for Bolinas.* Inverness: North Shore Books, 1973.

MASON, JACK, and HELEN VAN CLEAVE PARK, *The Making of Marin.* Inverness: North Shore Books, 1975.

OAKESHOTT, GORDON B., and CLYDE WAHRHAFTIG, *A Walker's Guide to the Geology of San Francisco.* San Francisco: California Division of Mines and Geology, 1966.

OLMSTED, NANCY, *To Walk with a Quiet Mind: Hikes in the Woodlands, Parks and Beaches of the San Francisco Bay Area.* San Francisco: Sierra Club Books, 1975.

TEATHER, LOUISE, *Discovering Marin.* Fairfax: Tamal Land Press, 1974.

WHITNAH, DOROTHY, *An Outdoor Guide to the San Francisco Bay Area: Exploring with Boots, Bikes, Backpacks, Buses, Boats, Books and BART.* Berkeley: Wilderness Press, 1976.

SAN FRANCISCO

Chapters 1 through 8

Although San Francisco contains less than one thirtieth of the GGNRA's acreage, these holdings have accounted for more than half of the park's publicity and controversy.

T his situation is logical enough: the San Francisco portions of the park are much better known than most of the Marin sections. After all, relatively few people—even among Bay Area residents—have ever hiked on Bolinas Ridge; but millions of people have visited the Cliff House. Furthermore, the San Francisco areas, many of which have been built up and extensively used for more than a century, offer more possibilities for alternative developments, and hence for controversy. Most people feel that Bolinas Ridge should probably be left pretty much as it is, but ask them what should be done with the ruins of Sutro Baths and you will get a wide

Out beyond the avenues, at Fort Funston on the beach, San Francisco looks almost bucolic

variety of strong opinions—everything from razing them entirely and encouraging the land to return to its natural state, to restoring them to their original grandeur. (San Franciscans tend to feel vehement about both their landscape and their historic structures.)

When the GGNRA took over seven of San Francisco's municipal parks in 1975, the Interior Department's top park official came to view them, and then went back to Washington and complained that the city had "unloaded . . . its broken-down parks" on the Federal Government. This charge met with an indignant response from then-Mayor Joseph Alioto, who said the shoreline property was "a priceless jewel that is being offered by the people of San Francisco without cost for the enjoyment of all Americans," and from then-San Francisco Park Manager Joseph M. Caverly, who asserted, "For their scenic value, these are the most precious waterfront properties of any city in the U.S." In the long run, Alioto and Caverly will surely be proved right. Nevertheless, the NPS does have its work cut out for it in some of these areas. Erosion is a constant problem at Lands End and on the south side of Sutro Heights. Dune-maintenance programs along Ocean Beach and at Fort Funston currently remain in limbo awaiting San Francisco's final decision on where and how to build its giant sewer. The Cliff House and environs are somewhat lacking in elegance, to put it kindly. However, the Park Service has already made one move to redeem its holdings: it has dismantled the tacky-looking fake rock that had been crumbling off of Sutro Heights across from the Cliff House. Perhaps the GGNRA, with its Federal funding, will be able to restore some other of these areas more successfully than the city's hard-pressed Department of Parks and Recreation.

Lumber schooner THAYER, now moored with other historic ships at the Hyde Street Pier

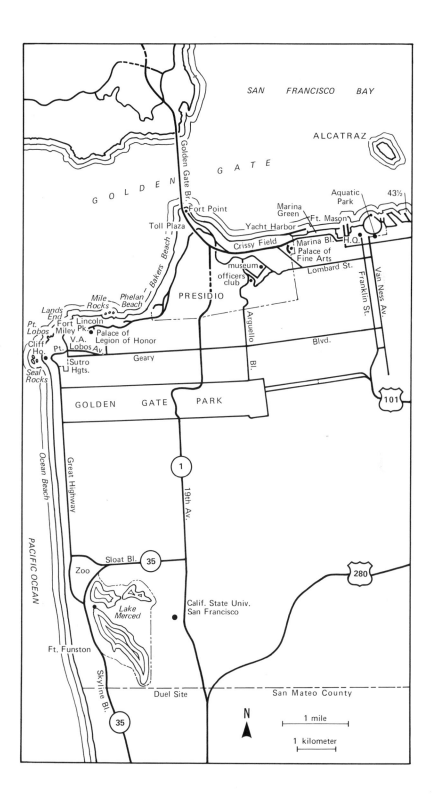

1. Fort Mason

HOW TO GET THERE

BY BUS: Muni #30 or 47 to Van Ness Avenue and Bay Street; walk 1 block west to Franklin Street.

BY CAR: Drive to the north end of Franklin Street.

FEATURES

Fort Mason is the place to start your explorations of the GGNRA. Not only does it contain the park's headquarters, but also it is a place well worth visiting for its own historic and scenic attractions—an enclave of timeless serenity amid the bustle of the City. San Franciscans who live nearby have long treasured it as a peaceful spot to spend an hour picnicking, ship-watching, strolling or bicycling.

Facilities: Water, restrooms, phones, picnic tables, a few grills (for charcoal only); guided tours Saturdays, Sundays and holidays at 1 p.m.; GGNRA headquarters open daily 8 a.m. to 5 p.m.

Phone: 556-0560

DESCRIPTION

Go first to the handsome, sprawling headquarters building, where you can find an assortment of maps and guides, plus up-to-date information on whatever is happening in the GGNRA. Pick up the leaflet *Fort Mason Discovery Walk,* even if you plan to take the guided tour.

The Spanish placed cannon here in 1797, three years after they built fortified Castillo de San Joaquin above what is now Fort Point to the west. The guns here, like those at Fort Point, never fired a shot in anger; in fact, the Spanish allowed them to fall into neglect. The Americans called the promontory Black Point, probably because it was then covered with dense laurel, which appeared dark from the Bay. (Most of the trees on the fort now are exotics that have been introduced over the past century and a quarter— some of them by John McLaren; those on the promontory are mainly Mon-

The headquarters of the GGNRA: a converted Army building at Fort Mason

terey cypress, toyon and eucalyptus.)

In 1850 President Millard Fillmore officially set the area aside for military use. However, the Army did not occupy it for several years, and meanwhile a number of squatters settled here, of whom the most prominent was General John C. Fremont. In the 1860s Colonel Richard Barnes Mason succeeded in dispossessing the squatters, and later the fort was named for him. (Fremont first challenged Mason to a duel, but later, instead, took the matter to court—where his side lost.)

Fortunately, four of the squatters' houses that date from 1855 remain today, albeit considerably modified, and they are still occupied by Army personnel. The southernmost one, which was extensively remodeled in the 1880s, now serves as the Officers' Club. As you walk north on Franklin Street, historic plaques describe these handsome houses, including the one where Senator David C. Broderick died after his duel with Judge David S. Terry.

On the west side of Franklin Street

Enjoying the view of the Bay from the promenade at Fort Mason

are several houses which the Army constructed between 1863 and 1890 to serve as enlisted men's quarters. Note that architecturally these houses are exactly what the Army was building during this period in the eastern United States: they show no trace of Spanish influ-

The Fort Mason Officers' Club; the original structure dates from 1855

Enjoying the Oceanic Society's "Save the Whale" exhibit at Fort Mason

ence, nor any acknowledgment that the climate of California might be different from that of, say, Massachusetts—their steeply pitched roofs are ideally designed for shedding several feet of snow! Note also the expanse of greenery around the houses: in land-poor San Francisco, only the military can afford such spaciousness! and so the sergeant at Fort Mason has a bigger lawn than the millionaire on Pacific Heights. (These two phenomena appear on a grander scale in the Presidio.)

At the north end of the fort, near where a plaque commemorates the old Spanish Bateria San Jose, you can pause to picnic or just enjoy the superb view of the Bay and its shipping. It is easy to understand why Fremont was so eager to defend his claim to this property.

You can continue to explore the fort at your leisure. You might want to visit Building 240 (north of head-quarters), which houses the San Francisco Bay Chapter of the Oceanic Society, a nonprofit organization devoted to the protection of the marine environment. Or you might want to take the stairway that leads down the eastern slope of the fort to Aquatic Park (described in Ch. 8). From this vantage point you can view the Bay fronts of the officers' quarters—prime real estate indeed, unless the constant bongo drumming at Aquatic Park gets on the residents' nerves.

Or you might head toward the three enormous piers at the northwest corner of the fort, which were Army transport docks for decades. During World War II more than 1½ million soldiers embarked from them. In 1962 the Army moved its transport facilities to Oakland. Since the GGNRA acquired Fort Mason, the future of these buildings has been the subject of much discussion and even, at times, controversy. All sorts of uses have

Picnicking near the old Spanish gun battery at Fort Mason

been suggested for the giant structures—as indoor tennis courts, theaters, art galleries, and so forth. A proposal to install a youth hostel in one of them aroused opposition among some Marina neighborhood groups, but the hostel will probably become a reality eventually. Meanwhile, the piers are being used for a variety of recreational and cultural projects, such as crafts fairs, science exhibits, dance classes and art shows. Indeed, Alfred Frankenstein, San Francisco's leading critic, has written: "What a wonderful opportunity that whole Fort Mason complex offers, now that it is part of the Golden Gate National Recreation Area! We ought to be spending our public money on the development of facilities there rather than on that Performing Arts Center downtown, which will benefit the New York concert managers more than the people of the Bay Region."

A group called the Fort Mason Foundation (headquartered in Building 310; phone 441-5705) has been formed to cooperate with the National Park Service to create a regional center with programs in the arts, humanities, recreation, education and ecology. Because of their enthusiasm, you can usually find some exciting activity going on in the pier area. If not. . .you can always try the Parcourse on the Marina Green (see Ch. 7).

Joggers enjoy the path above Fort Mason's old piers

2. Fort Funston

HOW TO GET THERE

BY BUS: At present there is no public transportation directly to the fort. Muni #70 runs counterclockwise around nearby Lake Merced. Muni #18 and L run to the Zoo; from there you can walk south on the beach a mile to the fort.

BY CAR: From Highway 1 (19th Avenue) go west on Highway 35 (Sloat Blvd.) and south on it after it turns into Skyline Blvd. for 1¼ miles to the entrance. Or take the Great Highway south to Highway 35 (Skyline Blvd.) and continue south ¾ mile to the parking lot on the right.

FEATURES

If you want to get an idea of what western San Francisco looked like before Henry Doelger covered it with row after row of pastel stucco boxlike houses, come to Fort Funston. Most of what is now the City was originally great sandhills like these.

Fort Funston is one of many parts of the GGNRA for which we can thank the military. It was established in 1898, during the Spanish-American War, as Laguna Merced Military Reservation, and in 1917 was renamed for Major General Frederick Funston, a hero of that war, who was in command of California during the 1906 quake and fire. For many years the area was off-limits to the public; as you walk around it you can still see the remains of old bunkers and roads left over from the days of military ownership.

Warning: Fort Funston is often windy.

Facilities: Privies, a few picnic tables. Hang gliding is permitted at Fort Funston subject to park regulations; for more information visit GGNRA headquarters at Fort Mason or phone 556-0560.

Regulations: "Please keep off iceplants."

DESCRIPTION

Some informal paths lead along the sand dunes southwest of the parking lot down to the beach. The 200-foot-high sand bluffs shield the beach-walker from sight and sound of the metropolis. Sometimes you will find you are

Fort Funston's massive Battery Davis, built just before World War II

Hang gliders at Fort Funston

The Fort Funston bluffs; looking south toward Mussel Rock, Point San Pedro and Montara Mountain

sharing the strand with only gulls, sandpipers, and an occasional equestrian. When the hang gliders meet at Fort Funston, on the other hand, you may enjoy the company of these gaily colored flying devices whirring overhead.

If you prefer to explore the dune area (and if it's not too windy), the logical place to head for is Battery Davis, ½ mile north of the parking lot. The "iceplant," or Hottentot fig, a species of mesembryanthemum which covers the dunes and which you are requested not to walk on, is a succulent that has been widely introduced in California as a ground cover, especially on road banks. An extremely hardy plant, it has spread all over the dune areas. You will also find native plants of the coastal sand-dune habitat, such as paintbrush,

lupine, buckwheat and lizard-tail.

Battery Davis was constructed in 1938. If you go through its tunnel and turn left, you soon come to an old paved road heading north over the dunes. From here a magnificent view spreads out over the western part of the city: the Golden Gate Bridge towers, the peculiar-looking Mt. Sutro television tower, Mt. Davidson with its cross, John McLaren Park and San Bruno Mountain—still bare of tract houses as this book goes to press, but the site of a prolonged controversy between conservationists and would-be developers. Below you spread the two sections of Lake Merced, divided by Harding Park Municipal Golf Course; and behind them the high-rises of Stonestown, San Francisco State University and Parkmerced.

Catching an updraft high above Fort Funston's beach

SIDE TRIPS

1-The four-mile path around Lake Merced is popular with joggers, bicyclists and birders. This fresh-water lake is fed by springs and protected from the ocean by the sandhills of Fort Funston. Although Lake Merced is an emergency reservoir for the City, boating and trout fishing are permitted here; for information phone 556-0300. Near the boat house is a picnic area with tables and grills, a bar and a small snack shop. If you are walking or biking around the lake, you may want to make a short side trip to the mini-park (no dogs allowed) at its south end which commemorates the Broderick-Terry duel of September 13, 1859. The entrance is near the Lake Merced Hill private tennis courts. A granite monument in a melancholy grove of eucalyptus and cypress notes that "the affair marked the end of dueling in California," and two granite shafts show where the participants stood. The dispute between U.S. Senator David C. Broderick and Chief Justice of the California Supreme Court David S. Terry arose out of the bitter political campaign of 1859; the two men belonged to differing factions of the Democratic Party. When you see how close the granite shafts are to each other, you can easily understand that Broderick was fatally wounded by a shot through the breast. (It's somewhat harder to understand how Broderick managed to miss Terry.) Broderick died three days later in one of the houses that are still standing at Fort Mason.

2-Beachcombers and geology buffs, as

Lake Merced and Harding Park

well as anyone looking for a brisk walk along an uncrowded shore near the sound and smell of the sea, may want to walk south a mile to Thornton State Beach or yet another two miles farther to Mussel Rock, which forms a natural barrier to southward beach travel. Walking along this southern stretch of Ocean Beach, which is known as Sand Dollar Beach, you may find either modern or fossil examples of that echinoderm. If you're truly a serious geology buff, before making this beach hike you will go to the State Division of Mines and Geology, in San Francisco's Ferry Building, and purchase for $.50 Oakeshott and Wahrhaftig's *A*

Walker's Guide to the Geology of San Francisco. This fascinating booklet contains a chapter called "Fleishhacker Zoo to Mussel Rock (Merced Formation)—A Plio-Pleistocene Nature Walk," complete with maps and diagrams showing, for example, where the San Andreas Fault comes in just above Mussel Rock.

3-The San Francisco State University campus is architecturally utilitarian, with one notable exception: the new Student Union completed in 1975 by architect Pafford Keatinge Clay. This extraordinary free-form mass of concrete is worth a visit—especially if you arrive in time to climb to the top just as the sun is setting over the ocean. It's a bit like climbing to the top of a Mayan or Egyptian pyramid.

4-The Zoo is, of course, perpetually delightful. It is open daily from 10 a.m. to 5 p.m. For complete information on fees for all ages, special facilities for the handicapped and for organized groups, feeding times for the various animals, and new developments, phone 661-4844 for a recorded message.

Between the Zoo and the Great Highway lie the melancholy remains of Fleishhacker Pool. Opened in 1925, this was the world's largest outdoor salt-water pool. Its 6 million gallons were piped in from the ocean and heated. In its palmy days it could accommodate thousands of swimmers at once.

3. Ocean Beach, Sutro Heights, the Cliff House and Sutro Baths

HOW TO GET THERE

BY BUS: Muni #2, 2X, 5, 38 and 38X to western end of lines; #18 to northern end of line.

BY CAR: From Highway 1 (Park Presidio) go west on Geary Blvd.; the main thoroughfare veers right at 39th Avenue onto Point Lobos Avenue, which runs past all these sites.

FEATURES

Few of the world's great cities are fortunate enough to be bordered by such a long stretch of sandy beach as San Francisco. Ocean Beach attracts crowds of sunbathers, flotsam gatherers, Frisbee throwers, equestrians and tourists. At the north end of Ocean Beach are three of the GGNRA's most fascinating and historic acquisitions: Sutro Heights, the Cliff House and the remains of Sutro Baths.

Regulations: As signs indicate, the dangerous undertow makes swimming and even wading highly inadvisable. However, bold surfers continue to chance the waves.

DESCRIPTION

The broad Great Highway, a combination seawall and road, runs above Ocean Beach for almost three miles. At times, during severe windstorms, the sand dunes threaten to reclaim their lost territory, and the highway has to be closed temporarily to autos until the drifted sand is cleared away. The future of the Great Highway is in some doubt; San Francisco is proposing to build a giant sewer under it, and the highway may be narrowed or even removed entirely.

For the best view down the beach, go to Sutro Heights Park. A trail leads up

Intrepid surfers off Ocean Beach

The early Cliff House, built in 1863 and destroyed by fire in 1894, viewed from Sutro Heights
(PHOTO, COURTESY GGNRA)

to it from the parking lot on Point Lobos Avenue across from Merrie Way; the main entrance (no cars) is at Point Lobos and 48th avenues. (The #2 and 2X buses stop here.) Adolph Sutro, an immigrant from Prussia, made his fortune by doggedly carrying out a great engineering feat—building a drainage and ventilating tunnel through a mountain to reach the silver of Nevada's Comstock Lode. With the proceeds from this venture, Sutro retired to San Francisco and bought up land in various parts of the City. It is to him that we owe the eucalyptus forest on the peak named after him—trees now dwarfed, alas, by the bizarre television tower that mounts guard like some Martian visitor.

Here on this cliff above the sea Sutro built a splendid mansion, where he entertained lavishly. The generous "King of the Comstock" allowed the public to walk and ride in his elaborate gardens. After his death his daughter, Dr. Emma Sutro Merritt, continued this policy, and she willed the estate to the City. Subsequently it was transferred to the GGNRA. Lamentably, the great

Adolph Sutro in his garden with his monkey
(PHOTO, COURTESY OF MARILYN BLAISDELL COLLECTION)

Victorian house is no more: it was condemned and torn down in 1939, the year after Dr. Merritt's death. But you can still walk freely in the overgrown remains of Sutro's formal garden, which is one of the pleasantest places in San Francisco on a sunny day. (Dogs are allowed on leash.)

The main carriage entrance at 48th and Point Lobos is guarded by two

Adolph Sutro's elegant Cliff House, built in 1896 and destroyed by fire in 1907

The present-day Cliff House, circa 1950 (PHOTOS, COURTESY GGNRA)

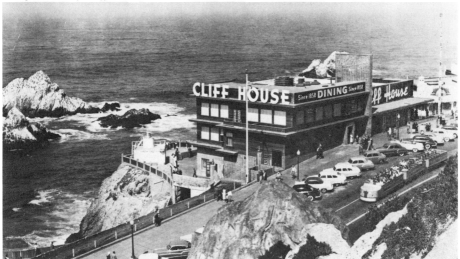

melancholy lions. One bears a weather-beaten plaque describing Sutro's career. As you walk along the path you pass a mutilated deer and a mutilated Diana. Sutro was a great tree-planter; the minor forest here includes the familiar Monterey cypress and many more exotic trees. (Incidentally, the three kinds of tree most conspicuously abundant in modern San Francisco—the Monterey cypress, the Monterey pine and the blue-gum eucalyptus—were all introduced into the City in the 19th Century. It is almost impossible to imagine now what San Francisco's landscape looked like before these trees were planted.)

Soon you arrive at a delightful green lawn with flower gardens and a white gazebo—a tempting place to spend a warm, lazy Sunday afternoon. However, for the great view, continue west. Here a battlement looks out over the Pacific from 200 feet above it and down the beach to Fort Funston. Just below you to the south are the vacant lots formerly occupied by Playland-at-the-Beach. This once-popular amusement park was razed to make room for an elaborate apartment complex, but the plan became enmeshed in a financial imbroglio before the first stone was laid, and at present this valuable ocean-front land remains empty. Beyond it is the west end of Golden Gate Park and two huge windmills, which have been armless for years but may eventually be restored.

Below you to the west is the Cliff House, looking somewhat more attractive from this distance than it does from closer up. The Cliff House is currently in its third, fourth or fifth reincarnation, depending on which historian you read. Everyone agrees that the first Cliff House was built in 1863 and was immensely popular with families during its first decade. After its vogue waned, however, it attracted a somewhat seedy clientele. In 1887 the Cliff House suffered severe damage when a ship loaded with dynamite was dashed against the rocks beneath it and exploded; and in 1894 the building burned to the ground. In 1896 Adolph Sutro, who had bought the Cliff House a few years before, constructed on the site the magnificent six-story Victorian gingerbread palace that appears in so many photographs of Old San Francisco. This Cliff House was even more popular and fashionable than the first one. Regrettably, after surviving the quake of 1906, it burned down in 1907. Sutro immediately replaced it with another, less spectacular structure—basically the one that exists today, although it has been remodeled over the years. Except for a hiatus during Prohibition, the Cliff House has remained an attraction for both tourists and natives over the years. The GGNRA

Adolph Sutro's Baths (constructed in 1896) in the days of their glory (PHOTO, COURTESY GGNRA)

acquired it in 1977 after lengthy negotiations.

At present, the Cliff House and adjacent structures house snack bars, restaurants, cocktail lounges, souvenir shops, a giant "camera obscura," and a Musee Mecanique full of coin-operated games. All these facilities are usually crowded. As at Muir Woods, tour buses pull up to disgorge enthusiastic visitors speaking languages one cannot even identify, much less understand! and everyone seems to be having a grand time.

From the cocktail lounges at the Cliff House and the terraces outside overlooking the ocean, you can often see and hear the pinnipeds that congregate on Seal Rocks offshore. Actually these noisy animals are not seals, but Steller's sea lions. (The Spanish called them sea wolves—*Lobos marinos*—from which derives the name of Point Lobos, San Francisco's westernmost point, a few hundred feet north.) They migrate down the coast 50 miles to Año Nuevo Island every summer to breed. When the sea lions are not in residence, the rocks are inhabited by huge flocks of cormorants.

Just north of the Cliff House lie the ruins of another of Sutro's contributions to San Francisco's turn-of-the-century good living, his wonderful Baths, built in 1896. A giant roof of colored glass housed six swimming pools holding water brought in from the ocean by an elaborate system of pipes and canals and heated to different temperatures. The popularity of Sutro Baths waned in the 1930s, and part of the structure was turned into an ice rink. The remaining pool was closed in 1952, and in 1966 the whole building burned to the ground in a spectacular fire.

The Baths' foundations remain as a fascinating, Roman-like ruin. Looking down on them, you see (and occasionally smell) an algae-covered pond which is the remains of one of the swimming pools. Signs warn of the

The present-day ruins of the Baths, which burned down in 1966; Fishermen's Rock and Seal Rocks in background

A busy day at Fishermen's Rock, just below the Cliff House

danger of venturing down the steep hillside through the jumbled concrete ruins, but there are a few obviously safe routes skirting the north and south rims of the basin. The northern route leads to a series of staircases and terraces which offer a breathtaking view of the Marin headlands. At low tide you can pick your way across the foundations of Sutro's pools. At the north end is a spooky tunnel with openings leading down to the sea. Near the south end a breakwater leads out to a rock popular with anglers.

Some people have suggested that the Baths and the Cliff House be restored to their original grandeur as they existed in Sutro's day. The Park Service has considered this possibility, but since it estimates the cost at a staggering $48 million—by far the most expensive alternative suggested for any portion of the GGNRA—such a restoration is unlikely to occur unless some very wealthy philanthropist develops an interest in the project.

The NPS has, however, made one step toward improving the area, by dismantling the artificial rocks on Sutro Heights across from the Cliff House. These rocks of concrete over a metal scaffolding have been there since the highway was widened in 1925. During the past decade they had begun to deteriorate noticeably. People occasionally camped overnight in them (illegally), and the smoke from their fires made an eerie sight as it drifted out of holes in the rock. Of course, since this is San Francisco, as soon as the Park Service began to talk of removing or rebuilding them, a Committee to Save Our Fake Rocks sprang up.

4. Lands End and Environs

HOW TO GET THERE

BY BUS: Muni #31 to Palace of the Legion of Honor on weekends and holidays; every day, Muni #2 and 2X to western end of line and 18 to northern end of line.

BY CAR: The most direct route is to take Geary Blvd. west to 34th Avenue and turn right. The most scenic route is to take Lincoln Blvd. through the Presidio and follow its continuation, El Camino del Mar, to the California Palace of the Legion of Honor.

FEATURES

Although the eroding cliffside at Lands End is not safe for exploring, two well-trodden routes contour along the bank and provide strollers with some of the most spectacular views in the City—or, indeed, the world. Both paths begin near the California Palace of the Legion of Honor, one of San Francisco's three major art museums. You can make a round-trip of a little over a mile starting at the museum. Or you can do the trip in reverse, starting at the parking lot in Merrie Way (see Chapter 3).

Facilities: Occasional picnic tables; coffee shop in museum basement. The GGNRA holdings here adjoin the Lincoln Park Municipal Golf Course. For information about playing on it, phone 221-9911.

Regulations: Dogs are not allowed in the museum or on the golf course.

A well-trod path along the bluffs at Lands End

The park authorities have posted signs warning against climbing on the steep, rapidly eroding cliffs. RESPECT THESE SIGNS. Every year a few foolhardy climbers fall to their deaths here.

DESCRIPTION

Get off the bus at the Legion, as it's colloquially known, or park in its lot. The semicircular terrace around the parking area is punctuated by four elegant lampposts designed by Arthur Putnam and featuring animals, pioneers and prospectors. They formerly adorned Market Street, but are much more appropriate in this elegant setting. One of the City's great views is from the balustrade looking east over the golf course toward downtown. A weatherbeaten obelisk below the balustrade is eccentric dentist Henry Cogswell's monument to "the Ladies' Seaman's Friend Society . . . a landmark of the seamen's last earthly port . . ." This monument serves to remind us of something many of the golfers may not be aware of: that Lincoln Park is built over a graveyard. The Chinese, the Italian and other ethnic groups' cemeteries were located here, and so was Potter's Field. The funereal aspect is echoed by Rodin's sculpture "The Shades," a monument to pioneer businessman and philanthropist Raphael Weill. On the north side of the balustrade a plaque bearing a rather puzzling inscription commemorates feminist Frances E. Willard.

The sumptuous museum building itself is George Applegarth's copy of the original Palace of the Legion of Honor in Paris. This one was a gift to San Francisco from Adolph B. and Alma de Bretteville Spreckels in memory of California's World War I dead. You enter past two equestrian statues by Anna Hyatt Huntington, statues of El Cid and Joan of Arc, and one of the five original bronze casts of Rodin's "The Thinker." The museum is open daily 10 a.m.-5 p.m.; age 18-64, $.75; 12-17, $.25; over 65, under 12 and the first day of the month, free. On Saturday and Sunday afternoons an organ concert takes place; the most interesting place, acoustically, to experience the music is not the room with the organ but the high-ceilinged square foyer.

To start the walk around Lands End, go down the paved road north of the museum (which is actually El Camino

Lincoln Park: a golf course built over a graveyard

Behind "The Thinker" at the entrance court of the California Palace of the Legion of Honor

The Presidio, Bakers Beach, Seacliff and Phelan Beach viewed from the cliffs of Lands End

del Mar) that ends at an automobile barricade. Taking the path through the barricade, you soon realize why El Camino had to be closed, for you traverse a landslide area. The semi-Mayan bulk of Fort Miley Veterans Administration hospital looms above you; the two Mile Rocks are visible below, and Point Bonita in the distant north. You will usually see young people and fishermen climbing over the cliffs—but I still don't recommend it.

After picking your way through the slide gully, where alyssum, radish and mustard flourish, you rejoin the twisted paving of El Camino. Here fennel grows more than head-high. Cypresses partly obscure the Bay view. Soon you come to the barricade that blocks El Camino from its southern end. During recent years, the trees just southwest of the barricade have been the site of a remarkable cat sanctuary. This situation originated when some of the retired persons who live in the neighborhood began feeding the feral cats of Lands End. As more cats were drawn to the area, their caretakers made in-

Exploring the old Ferries & Cliff House railroad grade that runs around Lands End

creasingly elaborate arrangements for them, providing tree houses and toys for them, in addition to gourmet delicacies. The benches adjoining the cat colony now serve as a social center for humans as well as felines.

Beyond the cat sanctuary is the main parking and view area of El Camino. From here you can look north to Marin and east to the Golden Gate Bridge. Here also is located the *U.S.S. San Francisco* Memorial—the actual bridge of this cruiser, which was riddled by gunfire during the Battle of Guadalcanal in November 1942. Although severely damaged, it managed to limp back to safety. Plaques tell the story, and list the 107 men who died during the action.

Turning your back to the memorial, you glimpse, on the cypress-covered hillside, a small, white tower—once the Marine Exchange lookout station. From here, news of incoming ships was telegraphed to the station on Telegraph Hill. Just south of the tower, a road leads up to the GGNRA portion of Fort Miley (see Side Trip at the end of this chapter).

The return trip is along the old right-of-way of the Cliff House & Ferries Railroad, which contours along the cliffs below El Camino del Mar and which was also disrupted by landslides. This roadbed is reached by a sandy path leading north from the Merrie Way parking lot, as well as by occasional paths leading down from El Camino. Cypresses obscure much of the Bay view until you reach a *Caution* sign under the *San Francisco* monument, where a break in the trees reveals the Mile Rocks below and the Marin headlands to the north. The view

Looking north from Lands End to the headlands of Fort Barry

remains sporadic as you pass on the right a concrete embankment currently covered with graffiti that are both literally and metaphorically colorful. Soon, yet another splendid panorama spreads before you, from the ocean to the Bridge and Angel Island. At low tide you may see the remaining wreckage of one of the ships that have come to grief on the rocks here, despite the installation of Mile Rock Light in 1906. Among them have been the tankers *Lyman Stewart* in 1922 and *Frank H. Buck* in 1937.

The route now runs across the slide area, passing some green serpentine rock, and rejoins the old railroad grade. At the next *Caution* sign, the path forks. The railroad bed continues contouring around the cliffs, crosses another slide area, and ends up at 32nd Avenue and El Camino del Mar. The more direct route back to the Legion is by the paved road, which leads uphill through a cypress grove and along the edge of the golf course. It ends near the monument to San Francisco's sister city, Osaka, Japan.

SIDE TRIP

Most of Fort Miley, which is a subpost of the Presidio, is occupied by the Veterans Administration hospital complex; but the GGNRA has made 12 acres available to the public (privies, picnic tables; no motorized vehicles; dogs on leash). The entrance is from the El Camino parking lot. The road leads past a chain-link fence to a large, grassy knoll, which offers a view south over the Sunset District and down the beach.

North of the knoll you can walk around the old bunkers and gun emplacements that formed part of the City's western fortifications. (Lt.-Col. John David Miley, for whom the fort is named, was one of the planners of the Golden Gate's defense system before he died of fever during the Spanish-American War.) This is a somewhat grim place for a picnic. However, if you climb to the top of the fort overlooking the Pacific, you will find a compass painted on the pavement, and in a pine-tree grove just north of it one of the City's most strategically located picnic tables.

5. Phelan Beach and Bakers Beach

HOW TO GET THERE

BY BUS: Muni #28 runs within a block of both beaches.

BY CAR: Phelan Beach is at the deadend of Seacliff Avenue, which can be reached either by taking 25th Avenue north, or Lincoln Blvd. west through the Presidio. Bakers Beach is at the deadend of Gibson Road just off Bowley Street, which makes an arc off Lincoln Blvd. near the southwest corner of the Presidio.

FEATURES

The GGNRA has acquired, on San Francisco's northwest corner, two beaches which are only a quarter of a mile from each other as the gull flies but which are separated by a portion of Seacliff, one of the City's most elegant residential communities. Phelan is a pocket beach; Bakers is much larger and offers more diverse recreational opportunities.

PHELAN BEACH FEATURES

This beach used to be called China Beach, after the Chinese fishermen who camped here. Former San Francisco Mayor and Senator James D. Phelan left $50,000 in his will to purchase it for the public, but after a protracted wrangle with the developers of Seacliff, the City and the state ended up paying another $160,000 for it in 1933.

Facilities: Restrooms

Regulations: No dogs

DESCRIPTION

If you didn't know this beach was here, you probably wouldn't happen upon it by accident! It is marked only by a wire fence across from the mansions at the end of Seacliff Avenue. Peering through the fence, you can see the beach and bathhouse at the bottom of the hundred-foot cliff. A gate in the fence gives access to an easy path leading down. The

Looking west from Bakers Beach to Seacliff and Lincoln Park

Battery Chamberlin at Bakers Beach: a gift from the Smithsonian Institution to the GGNRA

rather decrepit bathhouse contains toilets, changing rooms and lots of graffiti. Signs on the Bay side of it warn about the dangers of water pollution. However, nothing can spoil the magnificent view of the Marin headlands.

BAKERS BEACH
FEATURES

This mile-long beach is a delightful and usually uncrowded spot to refresh oneself amid the natural beauties of waves, sand and trees, plus a spectacular view of the Golden Gate—all within a block of a Muni bus stop! Author-naturalist Harold Gilliam, an aficionado of Bakers Beach, recommends it as a great place to observe in microcosm the interrelations of land and water that have shaped the City's shorelines.

Many writers say the beach is named for the same Col. Edward D. Baker who gave his name to the fort across the Bay, but Erwin Gudde, the authority on California place names, says it was named for the Baker family who owned the Golden Gate dairy ranch.

Facilities: Water, restrooms, picnic tables, grills (charcoal only), fire rings. Fishing is popular here, especially when the striped bass are running.

Regulations: No camping; dogs permitted on leash 9:30 a.m.-6:30 p.m.

Successful Bakers Beach fisherman with his striped bass

Watch out for the tide coming in!

DESCRIPTION

The main entrance to the beach on Gibson Road is near the southwest corner. A sturdy red brick building bearing the crest of the Army Corps of Engineers houses a pumping station. Walk past it to find the outlet of Lobos Creek, which in San Francisco's early days was a major source of water for the City and which for many decades has supplied the Presidio. It rises from a spring about a mile away. As the last remaining natural watercourse out of a dozen or so that once used to flow through the City, Lobos Creek is worth a visit. As Gilliam notes, ". . . its action on the sands of the beach, from tide to tide and season to season, illustrate the vastly larger landscape-shaping processes of streams and rivers everywhere."

Walking north along the beach, you pass the main parking lot and picnic area, sheltered in a grove of Monterey pines. These trees, like most of the ones in the Presidio, were planted here during the 19th Century. If you had been on the *San Carlos* when it was the first ship to enter the Bay, in 1775, you would have seen only a few willows on the sand dunes here.

Northeast of the picnic area in fenced-off Battery Chamberlin is a 95,000-pound cannon, a gift from the Smithsonian Institution to the GGNRA as a reminder of its historic past.

As you continue to walk north, you can clearly see the gray-green serpentine rock above Fort Point and the Golden Gate Bridge. If you want to take a side trip, a path leads up to the wooded bluff overlooking the beach.

At the northeast end of the beach is a rocky cove where, according to Gilliam, the sand may be as much as 15 feet higher in summer than it is in winter. You may want to return often to Bakers Beach to observe the changes wrought by the seasons.

6. The Presidio

MAP: In recent years the Presidio has been providing visitors a detailed map. You can pick it up at the Army Museum.

HOW TO GET THERE

BY BUS: Muni #28, 43 and 45.

BY CAR: There are several entrances, as a street map of San Francisco will show. One of the most frequented is the Lombard Gate, at Lombard and Lyon streets. Another is just south of the Golden Gate Bridge toll plaza—the last San Francisco exit before driving onto the bridge.

FEATURES

Although San Francisco's Presidio is not part of the GGNRA, it deserves mention in any guidebook to the Park. For one reason, it adjoins some of the most popular sections of the GGNRA. Furthermore, the Presidio—which must be one of the most urbane military posts in the world—has a long and honorable tradition of making its open space accessible to the community. Its 1400 acres offer hikers and bicyclists a unique opportunity to explore some of San Francisco's most historic and scenic facets. The whole post, in fact, was

Old Spanish cannon in Pershing Square, in front of the Presidio Officers' Club

Gun carriages and officers' quarters in the Presidio in the 19th century, before forestation
(PHOTO, COURTESY GGNRA)

made a National Historic Landmark in 1963.

Facilities: Restrooms in the museum.

DESCRIPTION

Begin at the Army Museum, near the intersection of Lincoln Blvd. and Funston Avenue and near the bus stops. The museum is in the oldest building on the post that was constructed by the U.S. Army, a hospital completed in 1857. It was remodeled in the 1970s and now offers a fascinating look at artifacts from San Francisco's military past (open Tuesday through Sunday, 10 a.m.-4 p.m.; free; no pets). Here you can also pick up maps for your future travels around the Presidio. In addition to the map mentioned above, which shows the main buildings and roads, the Army has issued two trail guides to the post. One outlines a 2-mile-long ecology trail and includes a key locating the various species of trees. The other outlines a 6-mile-long historic trail.

(You don't have to cover all 6 miles in one visit.)

Even if you don't feel like following one of these walks, you'll want to stroll around some of the historic sites. Walking south up Funston Avenue from the museum, you pass officers' quarters dating from around 1870. These delightful old frame buildings with their spacious lawns radiate the sort of serenity that we nostalgically associate with mid-19th century America. If it weren't for the palm trees, one might guess this was the Midwest. Actually, the area is probably much more attractive now than it was when the houses were built, because the Presidio was mostly sand dunes and desolate hills until the Army began a major forestation program in 1883. As we noted at Fort Mason, in land-hungry San Francisco only the military can afford sweeping lawns and acres of forest around their residences.

Turn right on Moraga Avenue to

Commanding General's quarters in the Presidio today, nestled in a mature eucalyptus forest

find the Roman Catholic Chapel of Our Lady, on the site where Father Palou said mass in 1776. Just beyond it

The trail winds through eucalyptus trees planted in the 1880s

is the Officers' Club, which incorporates part of the first building in San Francisco, the Presidio that Lt. Jose Joaquin Moraga laid out here in 1776. The WPA extensively remodeled the Officers' Club in 1934. Its entrance is flanked by two cannons from the Castillo de San Joaquin, the Spanish fort built in 1794 above the site of present-day Fort Point.

North of the Officers' Club is Pershing Square, named for World War I commander John "Black Jack" Pershing, who was earlier briefly in charge of the San Francisco Presidio. A plaque commemorates the tragic deaths of Pershing's wife and three daughters when their house here burned down. Pershing Square contains San Francisco's tallest flagpole, plus some more historic cannons. North of Pershing Square is the Main Parade Ground. Bordering it on the west is a handsome row of red brick barracks that date from around the turn of the century.

7. The Golden Gate Promenade

HOW TO GET THERE

BY BUS: Muni #19, 30 or 47 or Powell-Mason cable car to the east end; Muni #28 or any GGT bus to the Golden Gate Bridge toll plaza above the west end.

BY CAR: Drive to the north end of Franklin Street and park in Fort Mason; or park at the view-area lot just east of the San Francisco entrance to the Golden Gate Bridge (limit 6 hours).

FEATURES

This route along San Francisco's northern waterfront presents extraordinary diversity in its 3½ miles: magnificent vistas of the Bay and the Marin headlands; military structures spanning 125 years; upper-middle-class dwellings; beach, greensward and fishing piers.

The promenade route, which is marked by blue-and-white sailboat signs, runs between Fort Point and Aquatic Park, and if you take it in that direction—i.e., eastward—you will be starting at the oldest building and ending among some of the newest, in Ghirardelli Square and the Cannery; furthermore, you won't have to walk uphill at the end. On the other hand, if you cheat and start at Fort Mason you can pick up at GGNRA headquarters a free leaflet about the promenade that includes a map. The leaflet contains a lot of interesting historic lore about the sites along the route, so I recommend that you start at Fort Mason and pick it up. To get maximum enjoyment of the superb scenery, you can of course make it a round trip.

The Golden Gate Promenade is a popular bicycle route.

Facilities: Water, restrooms, picnic

Hopeful anglers frequent the beach along the Golden Gate Promenade

One way to keep in shape: follow the Parcourse along the Golden Gate Promenade

tables and phones at beginning and end and various places along the route.

DESCRIPTION

From GGNRA headquarters, head west through Fort Mason to Gashouse Cove at the foot of Laguna Street. (The enormous gas-storage tank that used to dominate this site has given way to apartment buildings.) Here begins San Francisco's yacht harbor. Two blocks northwest begins a popular recent addition to the Marina recreational scene, a Parcourse designed to test and improve one's physical fitness. Along its 2½-mile loop the Parcourse contains 18 stations with equipment for a variety of conditioning exercises—chin-ups, push-ups, and others more outre. If you want to display your prowess at "The Isometric Squat" before a group of admiring strangers, here's your chance! (Incidentally, there's another, less frequented Parcourse in Mountain Lake Park, just south of the Presidio.)

The Golden Gate Promenade and the Parcourse route continue on the seawall bordering the Marina Green. As you walk or jog along it, you can look out over the yachts to the bridge, the Marin headlands, Mt. Tamalpais, and Angel and Alcatraz islands. The Marina Green itself (like most of the district) is Bay fill dating from the 1915 Panama Pacific International Exposition. For several years it was used as an aircraft landing field, until nearby residents complained of the danger. During recent decades it has been a place where San Franciscans flock to engage in sunbathing, kite flying, boat watching, running and jogging. The Park Service has wisely recognized that these activities are indeed this area's highest and best uses, and has chosen to leave it as it is—except for the addition in 1976 of the Parcourse, which fits in well with the area's natural recreational features. Note, near the middle of the north side of the Green, Haig Patigian's sculptured monument to financier William C. Ralston, who swam to his death from today's Aquatic Park, a mile east of here.

Where the yacht harbor interrupts the Marina Green, the Golden Gate Promenade and the Parcourse continue along the old Belt Line railroad. On either side of you are symbols of the Good Life—fancy Mediterranean-style villas on your left and two yacht clubs plus some of the harbor's more opulent boats on your right. You can make a side trip here (if you're willing to take your life in your hand at the busy Baker

A little bit of New England by the Golden Gate

The granite stairs of old Fort Point

Street pedestrian crossing) to the Palace of Fine Arts, Bernard Maybeck's masterpiece and the one building remaining from the 1915 fair. It now houses the Exploratorium, a fascinating science museum full of do-it-yourself exhibits (open Wednesday through Sunday 1-5 p.m.; free, but donations welcome).

The Golden Gate Promenade turns north toward the Bay across the continuation of the Marina Green, the part most popular with sunbathers, past a windowless concrete storm-water-overflow building to some broad concrete stairs leading down to the Bay. To the east is the elegant St. Francis Yacht Club, much of which burned down just before Christmas 1976. The building was, in a sense, an indirect victim of California's drought: the fire started when a loose wire connected with a too-dry Christmas tree.

The next mile of the promenade runs along the shore edge of the Presidio and Crissy Field, which formerly accommodated planes and now accommodates helicopters. This portion of the route has to be one of the most unusual walks in the world, combining a wild variety of disparate features. On your right are a rough breakwater of jumbled concrete blocks, a sandy beach and the ever-changing vista of Bay, ships and bridge. To your left, behind a fence, is an Army parking lot; as you walk along you see Presidio buildings of diverse ages and styles, the freeway running over them, the rotunda of Maybeck's Palace, the mansions of Pacific Heights and the Presidio's forest in the background—and, of course, that unique landmark, the Mt. Sutro television tower. And under your feet are plentiful specimens of the state flower, California poppy. (Indeed, botanists have designated the Presidio as the type locality for this plant.)

Beyond Crissy Field is the Promenade Classroom, where Ida Geary, author of *The Leaf Book*, has for several years

Two historic structures on the Golden Gate: Fort Point (1861) and the Bridge (1937)

been giving free classes in plant identification and plant printing. (To find out about these, phone San Francisco Community College, 239-3076, or Fort Point, 556-1693.) Next you pass the Coast Guard station, a charming enclave of New England Victoriana amidst its utilitarian Army surroundings.

The Golden Gate Promenade jogs around a jeep/truck parking lot and arrives at an always-popular pier where anglers fish for perch and crabs. Just beyond are two recycled, repainted Army buildings which the Park Service is using for office and classroom space. The last few hundred yards are along a seawall where on windy days ocean spray blows into walkers' faces. The cliffs above Fort Point and the southern end of the Golden Gate Bridge contain large quantities of serpentine, the official state rock (see Chapter 21). Amateur botanists can find a wide variety of plants, both native and introduced, on these cliffs.

As you approach Fort Point, make a short detour to the plaque that describes how it—like so many other military artifacts—proved to be obsolete almost as soon as it was built! The old brick fort is now a National Historic Site and is open free daily from 10 a.m. to 5 p.m. The rangers will give you a historical leaflet about the building, and you can take a guided tour around it. In recent years the fort has been the site of some memorable Dixieland jazz concerts; those high, thick brick walls make for some interesting acoustic effects.

Now you can retrace your steps along the promenade, appreciating on your eastward trip the views of Fort Baker, Tiburon, Angel Island, Alcatraz, the Berkeley Hills, Mt. Diablo, the Bay Bridge and the San Francisco skyline. Or you can reach public transportation by taking the paved path that starts at the marked pedestrian crossing and leads uphill under the bridge. When you near the top, head for the gate in the green fence. It will bring you out behind the statue of Joseph Strauss. To catch a GGT bus heading for downtown San Francisco, you have to take the pedestrian walkway under the bridge. Note that there are two bus-stop kiosks on the west side of the toll plaza: the one nearest the freeway is for GGT, the one in the parking lot for Muni #28.

Surfing off Fort Point; only place inside the Golden Gate where this is possible

8. Aquatic Park and Environs

HOW TO GET THERE

BY BUS: Muni #19, #30, #32 and #47; the Hyde Street cable car comes here too, if you can get on it. (Most San Franciscans consider the cable cars purely a tourist attraction, not a means of transportation.)

BY CAR: Drive to the foot of Van Ness Avenue or Columbus Avenue; unless you're lucky, you'll probably end up in a pay lot or garage.

FEATURES

The Aquatic Park-Ghirardelli Square-Cannery area is where you want to take your great-aunt from Wichita, your lover from Stockholm, or anyone else who's visiting the Bay Area. It's also a fine place to take your godchildren from the Sunset District, or to visit by yourself when you feel like being entertained or amused—or even educated and inspired (but *not* when you feel like being alone).

Facilities: Everything imaginable except parking spaces.

DESCRIPTION

If you approach Aquatic Park from Fort Mason (see Ch. 1), you descend past two big water tanks and a rather elegant, vaguely mission-style auxiliary pumping station built after the 1906 earthquake and fire. Beyond it is the old pier that once served Alcatraz, now decorated with wildly colorful murals painted by schoolchildren.

The 1850-foot-long curving Municipal Pier is a product of the Depression years; the WPA dug out the lagoon and created the beach here in the late '30s. The walk out the windswept pier is definitely worth the trip, in order to watch the anglers and their catch and to get a unique view of the diverse architecture on San Francisco's northern waterfront: the strictly utilitarian tan Kodak Building, the quintessentially '30s white Maritime Museum, the red-brick Victorian clock tower of Ghirardelli Square and, forming a backdrop, the curved slabs of the Fontana apartment buildings. The

The old Alcatraz pier and the curving Municipal Pier

WPA workers in 1937 building the "People's Palace" that eventually became the Maritime Museum (PHOTO, COURTESY GGNRA)

Fontana buildings actually have some historical and environmental interest: these slabs so outraged the Russian Hill dwellers whose views they blocked that they inadvertently triggered an anti-highrise movement that led to the imposition of a 40-foot height limitation on waterfront buildings.

Turning back, as you head south from the pier toward the bleachers, you pass on your right a mini-park constructed by a youth conservation corps, and the tunnel for the old State Belt Line Railroad, which ran along the Embarcadero and under Fort Mason to the Presidio. Passing the circular restroom-snackbar building, which obviously matches the Maritime Museum, bear left on the railroad track. A huge pylon containing a loudspeaker is another heritage of the '30s. Behind it are bocce ball courts, always full of Italian men playing their game, obliv-

Aquatic Park rowing clubs, Haslett Warehouse and the skyline of San Francisco as seen from one of the historic vessels at the Hyde Street Pier

The Maritime Museum today, with the curved slabs of the controversial Fontana apartment buildings in the background

ious of the commotion around them.

The shiplike white Maritime Museum (architects William Mooser Sr. and Jr.) is one of the finest examples of Streamlined Moderne architecture in the City. It is altogether fitting that a building in this style, which emphasizes nautical motifs, should house such a museum. However, when the WPA commissioned it they had no such intention; they planned it to be a "people's palace," or casino. They also built in changing rooms to accommodate 5000 swimmers!—about 4990 more than actually swim in the chilly Bay on any day. It was only by a happy accident that this building was available in the late '40s when a group of enthusiasts decided that San Francisco should have a permanent museum devoted to its maritime history. Its great collection of nautical art and artifacts will enthrall history buffs and shiplovers of all

ages (open daily 10 a.m. to 5 p.m.; adults, $1.00; age 12-17, $.50; 65 and over, $.25; children through 11 and members, free). Note the sculptured murals flanking the front door by Sargent Johnson (the only Black artist in the Bay Area's WPA program) and the *Undersea Life* murals inside by Hilaire Hiler.

The bleachers were another WPA Depression project. On all except the most stormy days they are inhabited by picnickers, sunbathers and congo drummers; and a few hardy souls (some of them well over 60) may often be seen here emerging from a swim in the Bay. One who did not emerge was William C. Ralston, who in 1875 swam to his death from here on the day after his Bank of California failed. A monument to Ralston is on the Marina Green, a mile west.

The next great attraction on the

Ruth Asawa's popular mermaid fountain in Ghirardelli Square

route is Ghirardelli Square. This fascinating urban treasure is a monument to the taste, imagination and public spirit of William Matson Roth, who saw how an old factory building could be transformed into an enticing complex of shops, restaurants, bars, theaters and plazas. A lesser man would simply have razed the old chocolate and woolen factories and erected a concrete box in their place. It is a tribute to Ghirardelli Square's charm that more natives than tourists visit it (unlike nearby Fisherman's Wharf), and keep coming back. Roth, in making his vision a reality, had the help of Wurster, Bernardi & Emmons, architects, and Lawrence Halprin & Associates, landscapers. The original factory buildings, which were a model for their time, were designed by William Mooser, Sr., who later collaborated with his son on the totally different Maritime Museum building.

To get a map of the Ghirardelli complex, visit the information kiosk in Fountain Plaza. Don't miss Ruth Asawa's delightful mermaid fountain nearby.

Return to Beach Street and Victorian Park, passing along the way a gaggle of street musicians and crafts hawkers. At the foot of Victorian Park are three rowing clubs which are currently embroiled in hassles with the City park department, over their lease, and with a group of feminist lawyers, over their refusal to admit women. Adjoining them is another Streamlined Moderne restroom, somewhat the worse for wear.

On the east side of Hyde Street is a huge old red brick building, the Haslett warehouse, currently called the Wharfside, which the GGNRA took over in 1977. Much debate has centered on the future of this building. Many people think it should house a grand museum—sort of a Smithsonian West—devoted to transportation by rail or ship or both.

At the corner of Hyde and Beach streets is the cable-car turntable, in front of which a long line of tourists is

The long wait in Victorian Park for the Hyde Street cable car

usually waiting patiently to board. If you feel like taking a cable car downtown, you might try walking 3 blocks east to Taylor Street, where you can catch an identical, equally authentic cable car with a much shorter wait. If you want to go downtown with no wait, just catch the #19 bus here.

If you want to continue to amuse yourself in this area, various possibilities beckon, according to your age and inclinations:

1-You can go the Buena Vista (southwest corner of Beach and Hyde) and try to squeeze in. The BV is the bar where, supposedly, *Chronicle* columnist Stanton Delaplane introduced Irish Coffee to the United States. Another *Chronicle* columnist, Charles McCabe, has cited it

as a classic illustration of Yogi Berra's dictum, "Nobody goes there anymore—it's too popular." The BV is still a very pleasant bar at about 10 a.m. on a weekday.

2-You can walk down to the Hyde Street Pier and climb aboard three old schooners and a ferry that holds autos from the '20s (open daily 10 a.m.-6 p.m.; $.50; age 62 and over, and 15 and younger, free.)

3-You can walk down Beach Street to 633, the Christian Brothers Wine Museum of San Francisco (open Tuesday through Saturday 11 a.m.-5 p.m., Sunday noon to 5 p.m., closed Monday; free; no tasting). Here is a unique collection of drinking vessels and graphic art on every aspect of the making and

Bocce ball courts at Aquatic Park

enjoyment of wine. The handsome interior is by Gordon Ashby; those who have visited the Oakland Museum will recognize his touch in the inscriptions painted on the roof beams.

4-Across the street from the Wine Museum is the Cannery, Leonard V. Martin's shopping-restaurant complex built in emulation of Roth's Ghirardelli Square. This was originally the cannery of the Del Monte Fruit Company, whose logo of a star in a circle has become the Cannery's emblem. The exterior of the old red brick building was painstakingly saved; the interior was completely gutted and an enticing multi-level array of stores and plazas constructed (Joseph Esherick, architect). A series of photographs on the lower level shows how it was done. Undoubtedly it would have been cheaper to tear the whole building down and start from scratch. San Francisco, and the nation, can be thankful to Roth and Martin for showing us how to recycle old industrial buildings into delightful urban marketplaces and meeting places. These men are the 20th-century counterparts of the public-spirited Adolph Sutro, or even the Medici family in Renaissance Florence.

In the pilot house of historic ferryboat EUREKA, at the Hyde Street Pier

Wandering through the ever-fascinating Cannery

THE BAY

Chapters 9 through 11

San Francisco Bay is, in a sense, the reason for the existence of the GGNRA because its great strategic value led the military to set aside the headlands on either side of its entrance, the Golden Gate, and thereby preserve them in the public domain.

When you stand on the cliffs above Fort Point or Kirby Cove and look out over the Golden Gate, it is hard to believe that for two centuries explorers sailed past it without noticing it. Yet so they did—unless Francis Drake actually entered it in 1579, as some historians believe. (The controversy over just where in California Drake landed is still raging fiercely 400 years after the event.) It was left to an overland expedition led by Gaspar de Portola to discover the Bay in 1769.

San Francisco Bay, including its northern extension, San Pablo Bay, is

The Golden Gate and its maritime traffic, viewed from Mt. Caroline Livermore on Angel Island

about 55 miles long and 3 to 12 miles wide. It is by far the largest harbor on the Pacific Coast and one of the greatest in the world. As Father Juan Crespi, annalist of the overland expedition that discovered it noted, "This port . . . could contain not only all the armadas of our Catholic Monarch but also all those of Europe."

Today, two great forces operate within the Bay: the Pacific Ocean and the Sacramento-San Joaquin river system. Twice each day the ocean tide floods in through the Golden Gate and ebbs out of it; the volume of water that flows through the Gate four times each day averages about 1,250,000 acre-feet, or about five million acre-feet total. (An acre-foot is the amount of water re-

Anglers at Fort Baker's Horseshoe Bay piers enjoy a grand view of the City and the Bay Bridge

quired to cover an acre to a depth of one foot.) Meanwhile, fresh water is constantly entering the Bay from the river system. The runoff from the Sierra Nevada drains into the Central Valley to form the two rivers, the Sacramento and the San Joaquin, which join in the Delta just west of Stockton and pass through Carquinez Strait to the Bay. The rivers carry with them huge quantities of sediment, perhaps 13,800 tons per day, most of which is deposited in the Bay. The hiker on Mt. Tamalpais or Angel Island can often, especially in spring, look down on fascinating, constantly changing water patterns as the visibly muddy river currents encounter the incoming ocean tide.

Sedimentation was even greater a few decades ago: it took the river system about fifty years to purge itself of the debris deposited by hydraulic gold-mining that went on in the Sierra from the 1850s until 1884. (In that year angry farmers downstream finally succeeded in getting a court order that virtually halted hydraulic mining.) As a result of continual sedimentation, both natural and man-made, 75 per cent of the Bay, excluding the Golden Gate area, is less than 18 feet deep, and its bottom is more of an ooze than a solid floor. The Army Engineers maintain the main channels at 50 feet; the channel through the Golden Gate, the Bay's deepest, is about 350 feet deep.

When the Spaniards discovered the Bay in 1769, it covered 700 square miles. Since then—and especially since the gold rush of 1849—extensive filling and diking along the shores have reduced its area to a little over 400 square miles. By the early 1960s, continued filling threatened to reduce the Bay to a narrow, polluted, foul-smelling channel. At this point many citizens became alarmed and started a grass-roots movement to save the Bay. Their concern resulted in the formation of the Bay Conservation and Development Commission (BCDC), a regional organization that has been remarkably successful in regulating building, filling and other activities along the shore.

9. Across the Golden Gate Bridge to Sausalito

HOW TO GET THERE

BY BUS: San Francisco Muni #28 bus or any GGT bus to the toll plaza.

BY CAR: This trip is ideally suited to public transit; but if you wish to drive, proceed to the bridge by Highway 101 or Highway 1 and park in the view area just southeast of the toll plaza (limit 6 hours).

FEATURES

The Golden Gate Bridge is one of the great engineering triumphs of the 20th century, and one of the most successful marriages of technology and esthetics ever. Walking across it is one of those "only in San Francisco" experiences that cannot be duplicated anywhere else in the world—something every Bay Arean should try at least once.

Having said all this, I feel obliged to point out that although the walk across the bridge is unique, exhilarating and scenically spectacular, it is not an un-alloyed delight: while it gratifies the sight, it assaults the other senses. Gusty, chilly winds frequently blow through the Golden Gate. Furthermore, the constant vehicular traffic is both noisy and smelly, and it shakes the bridge in a manner that is a bit unnerving to those of us who have gone through a few earthquakes. After a mile and a half of these sensations, it is relaxing to reach terra firma at Vista Point. To continue on via Fort Baker to Sausalito, as described below, adds about 2½ miles, more downhill than up.

Regulations: The east sidewalk is open daily from sunrise to sunset to pedestrians, free; the west sidewalk is open weekends and holidays to bicyclists, free; on weekdays, bicyclists must use the east sidewalk. In the spring of 1977 the bridge-district directors banned bicycle-riding on the span after two injured cyclists sued the district. However, they rescinded the ban when 500 outraged bicyclists showed up at their next meeting. They have placed signs on the bridge warning bicyclists of the dangers, especially around the towers.

Some people like to bicycle across the Golden Gate Bridge . . .

. . . while others prefer to stroll and savor the view

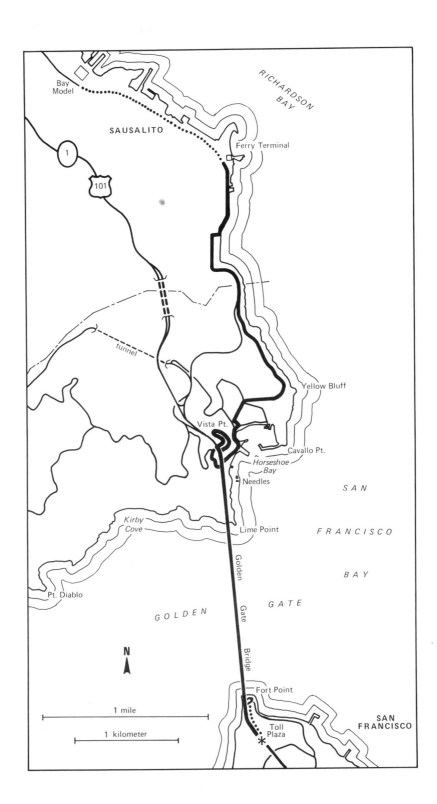

DESCRIPTION

From the east side of the toll plaza, take the pedestrian subway under the plaza to the headquarters of the Golden Gate Bridge, Highway and Transportation District. Here you can pick up the most recent schedules and a pamphlet that will tell you everything you ever wanted to know about the bridge—indeed, possibly more than you ever wanted to know about it, unless you are an engineer.

Retrace your steps along the subway and walk down to the statue of Joseph B. Strauss, the engineering genius who managed to convince the people of San Francisco and the North Bay, despite a lot of well-financed opposition, that such a bridge could and should be built. Behind the statue a paved, then gravel road leads down to historic Fort Point (see Chapter 7).

As you start walking on the bridge, you can look down on the massive brick fort. A sign points out the illegality of "dropping or throwing any object or missile from a toll bridge," and warns that this sidewalk is under television surveillance. The railing on the section of the east sidewalk above the fort now is surmounted by a high wire fence. Such a fence may eventually run all the way across the bridge, to deter would-be suicides. (So far over 600 persons are known to have jumped to their deaths from it.)

As you proceed across, you may want to pause frequently to take in the incomparable panorama: the Pacific Ocean, the San Francisco skyline, the Bay Bridge and Treasure Island, the East Bay cities, Alcatraz and Angel islands and the Marin headlands. Adding liveliness to the scene may be

Fog rushing through the Golden Gate fascinates Hawaiian tourists at Vista Point

LEGEND

*⤳	. . . . Hiking Trail Routes
—①—	. . Car Access Road or Highway
••••••••••	. . . . Side Trip
– – – – –	. . . . . . Alternate Trail Routes
— — —	. . . . Park Boundaries
—·—·—·	. . . . City Limits
⌇⌇⌇	. . . . Creeks and Streams
≈≈≈	. . . . Shoreline
△ ■ ● ○	. . . Points of interest or places mentioned in the text.

Lime Point viewed from the Golden Gate Bridge

Fort Baker around the turn of the century—before tree-planting
(COURTESY RICHARD H. DILLON)

sailboats, tugs, tankers, freighters, or passenger liners. If you are hiking on a weekday, you will probably pass some of the workmen who are engaged in the continuous job of repainting 10 million square feet of bridge its distinctive International Orange.

As you pass the second tower, you enter Marin County. The tower is just above Lime Point, where a lighthouse has operated since 1900. Like most of the lighthouses in the Bay, it is now automated. Just to the north are the Needles, sharp rocks covered, like Lime Point, with guano. Your walk across 8981 feet of bridge ends at Vista Point on your right (water, restrooms, phones). Except in the middle of a howling blizzard, the parking area and promenade here are always full of tourists from every part of the globe, busily photographing one another in

front of the spectacular San Francisco skyline.

At the northwest end of the parking area, across from a sign *San Francisco through underpass,* bear right on a graveled road that curves east to overlook Fort Baker. This is the oldest of the three military reservations that occupy the Marin headlands, the others being Forts Barry and Cronkhite to the west. All are named for old soldiers who have otherwise faded away—this one for Colonel Edward D. Baker, who fell in one of the early battles of the Civil War. (Although California was two thousand miles from most of the battlefields, a surprising number of landmarks in the Bay Area commemorate heroes of that conflict.)

The graveled road twists under the bridge to join paved Conzelman Road (no sign). Continue downhill on it,

Fort Baker today: same buildings as photo at left

Looking northeast toward Tiburon and Raccoon Strait from the Fort Baker headlands

along a bank full of rather scruffy vegetation (coyote brush, broom, lupine, sage, fennel, etc.). The road bears east to go under the bridge again and soon arrives at Horseshoe Bay, a sheltered spot much favored by fishermen. It would also be favored by all those photographers up at Vista Point, if they knew about it: the view of San Francisco and the bridge from this angle just above Bay level is unique.

After exploring Horseshoe Bay, head north toward the broad expanse of the Fort Baker parade ground. You may want to walk around it to enjoy the turn-of-the-century wooden buildings. The old fort, like so many of the former military properties that have come into the GGNRA, now conveys a feeling of tranquility; it's a little enclave of the past just minutes from roaring Highway 101.

Leave the parade ground by the paved road heading east, passing the post library on the left and soon the remains of old bunkers on the right, overlooking the Bay. As you walk along the road, most of which has a comfortably wide shoulder, you have ever-changing views of the city, the islands, Belvedere and, as you curve north, Sausalito. A short mile from the fort, the main access road from Highway 101 comes in from the left. You have to walk along the edge of this narrow road for a few hundred yards, but soon you reach sidewalk.

Along the approach to Sausalito are

Fishing from Sausalito's Bridgeway

Ferryboat GOLDEN GATE passing Angel Island on its way to San Francisco from Sausalito

a number of picturesque buildings from its early days. From 1838 to 1868 the area was part of Rancho Saucelito, granted to the English sailor William A. Richardson. After his death the Saucelito Land and Ferry Company started subdividing the property and operating ferry service from San Francisco. The North Pacific Coast Railroad took over the ferry in 1875, and from then until the building of the Golden Gate Bridge, Sausalito was not only a commuter haven but also a gateway to the rest of Marin County. Among the more splendid remnants of the past century is the building you pass at 201 Bridgeway dating back to the 1870's, which is now occupied by Sally Stanford's Valhalla Restaurant.

Parallel sidewalks run along the Bay side of Bridgeway, one just above water level. Occasional benches beckon you to rest and enjoy the always-spectacular view. Soon after passing a bronze seal sculpted by Al Sybrian, you arrive at downtown Sausalito. The once peaceful little commuter village, which became a shipbuilding center in World War II, is now one of the Bay Area's major tourist attractions. On weekends its sidewalks, shops, bars and restaurants teem with visitors who run the gamut from ultra-hip to ultra-straight. If you enjoy people-watching or browsing through boutiques and craft shops, you can while away a pleasant afternoon in Sausalito. When you get hungry or thirsty, you can repair to any of a wide variety of establishments that cater to almost every taste.

At the center of town is a tiny park, Viña del Mar Plaza, named for Sausalito's sister city in Chile. On the Bay side of the plaza is the dock for the *Golden Gate*, which plies to the Ferry Building in San Francisco. This scenic half-hour boat ride is a delightful way to get back to the City. If you prefer to stick with the bus, you can pick one up at any of the signed stops on Bridgeway.

SIDE TRIP

A visit to the U.S. Army Corps of Engineers' model of the San Francisco Bay and Delta is another adventure that every Bay Arean should experience at least once. You can reach it by walking a mile north on Bridgeway from central Sausalito. Along the way you pass the yacht harbor and several businesses devoted to boats and their accoutrements.

A cavernous two-acre shed at 2100 Bridgeway houses the hydraulic model, which is built to a horizontal scale of 1 foot = 1000 feet and a vertical scale of 1 foot = 100 feet. Over a hundred thousand gallons of water flow through the model to simulate in 14.9 minutes one tidal cycle of a lunar day, or 24 hours 50 minutes. The visitor, feeling like Superman, can wander on bridges and balconies above the relief map of the area from the Golden Gate to Sacramento, while observing the action of tides and river currents.

The model is open free on weekdays from 9 a.m. to 4 p.m., and currently on the first and third Saturdays of each month during the same hours. Because the Saturday opening hours are subject to change, it is advisable to phone 332-3870 to confirm them. GGT buses stop near the model; you can pick one up for your return trip.

Tiburon, Raccoon Strait and Angel Island as they appear in the Army Corps of Engineers' working model of the Bay and Delta

10. Alcatraz

HOW TO GET THERE

The only way to get to the island is on ferries operated by Harbor Carriers. Except during summer, you can make advance reservations for tours by phoning 546-2805 two or more days in advance. Between Memorial Day and Labor Day, trips are on a first-come, first-served basis: tickets for the day go on sale at 8 a.m. and are usually sold out by 9:30. The boats leave from Pier 41 beginning at 9 a.m. and every half hour thereafter in summer, slightly less often in other seasons. Fees: adults, $2; age 5-12, $1; under 5, free. The boat fee includes the island tour. The entire tour, including boat ride to and from the island, takes about two hours.

Pier 41 adjoins Fisherman's Wharf, one of San Francisco's main tourist attractions, so parking can be tricky. Muni #15, #19 and #32 run to Pier 41; so does the Powell & Mason cable car, if you can get on it.

FEATURES

Alcatraz probably exerts the most fascination on tourists of any part of the GGNRA. Even though the last prisoners were removed from The Rock in 1963, its brutal history continues to flicker across late-night TV screens around the world.

Because of both its checkered career and its unique setting, Alcatraz has prompted more, and more diverse, suggestions for its future than any other part of the GGNRA. The island has been proposed as a site for: a youth hostel; a honeymoon haven; a nudist camp; a gambling casino; a monument to the founding of the United Nations; a Disney-like "Prisonland"; and "an experimental, self-sufficient colony deriving its energy from wind, tide and sun, growing and raising its own food, and deriving fresh water and salt from the sea." A few purists have suggested that the island simply be restored to its

Alcatraz as the tour boat approaches it; sightseeing helicopter near the light house

Alcatraz during its career as "The Rock"—the tightest-security Federal penitentiary in the nation (PHOTOS, COURTESY GGNRA)

Alcatraz during its 19-month occupation by Native Americans (PHOTO, COURTESY GGNRA)

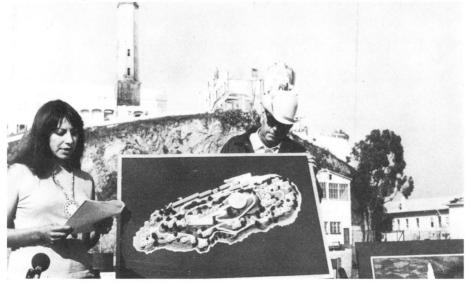

natural state—a nearly bare rock of sandstone and serpentine. (It was never, incidentally, a habitat for flocks of pelicans—*Alcatraces*. Captain Ayala in 1775 gave the name *Isla de Alcatraces* to what we now call Yerba Buena Island; then a subsequent mapmaker misapplied it to the smaller, barren island.)

The Park Service, besieged by conflicting proposals, has wisely decided to postpone the final decision on Alcatraz for a few years and concentrate instead on developing less controversial portions of the GGNRA. Meanwhile, the rangers conduct excellent historic tours of the island in its present state.

Facilities: On the boat, restrooms and snack bar; on the island, four privies.

Regulations: No pets. Comfortable walking shoes and extra jacket strongly advised.

DESCRIPTION

As the tour boat approaches the island, you get a good view of the lighthouse, the oldest one on the Pacific Coast. It began operation in 1854. The present structure dates from 1909. Like all the lighthouses in the Bay, it is now completely automated, flashing its revolving light every five seconds, day and night. As the boat approaches the dock, you can still see (as this book goes to press) the large sign lettered on the water tower: WELCOME - INDIAN LAND. This greeting dates from the 19-month period in 1969-71 when a group of Native American activists occupied the island, which at that point was in a sort of bureaucratic limbo. Federal marshals finally evacuated the remains of the dissension-ridden colony after the lighthouse was damaged in a

Alcatraz tour boat docks at "The Rock" while sightseers on a bay cruise boat look on

fire, and the light allowed to go out.

The landing place is near the oldest fortifications on the island, which date back to the 1850s. The fortress on Alcatraz and the gun batteries on Angel Island formed the inner defenses of San Francisco Bay, designed to protect it against any naval invader that might

This gull made the trip from Alcatraz to the mainland; did any of the prisoners?

get past the guns of Fort Point and Lime Point. (Apparently the Spanish had never considered fortifying the two islands.)

Alcatraz's career as a prison site began in 1859. In the early days the Army used it for holding Indians, Confederates and deserters. The island did not gain its great fame as "The Rock," however, until it became a Federal civilian prison in 1934—designed as a maximum-security penitentiary for hard-core incorrigibles from *other* prisons. The guided tour will give you a very graphic view of what life was like for the inmates here, and how nearly impossible it was to escape from The Rock (although a few men may have made it). For a real thrill of horror, you can shut yourself in "the hole" for a minute.

A tour group gets a small impression of maximum security prison life in the main cell block

11. Angel Island

HOW TO GET THERE

BY BOAT: Ferries run to the island from San Francisco's Pier 43, the Berkeley Marina and the Tiburon dock. For schedules and fares, phone: San Francisco and Berkeley, 398-1141; Tiburon, 435-2131.

MAP: Trail map available from headquarters.

FEATURES

Angel Island, which covers about one square mile, is the largest island in the Bay. It is a delightful place to escape for a day from the bustling world of cities and automobiles. Instead of struggling on a smoggy freeway to get to your trailhead, you can relax on a breezy boat ride; and when you get there you can enjoy historic buildings, oak woodlands, and some of the most exciting views of any place in the Bay Area.

As this book goes to press, Angel Island is still a state park, but it may be turned over to the GGNRA whenever the state's governor so determines. Consequently the NPS has included the island in its long-range planning.

Facilities: Water, restrooms, picnic tables and grills (charcoal may be purchased at headquarters) at Ayala Cove; tables scattered around other parts of the island; organized groups can reserve the playing field and picnic facilities at East Garrison up to 90 days in advance. During summer, concessionaires operate a snack bar and elephant trains. Fishing is possible at various places on the island. Private boats may use the boat slips and moor overnight on the buoys. The ferries carry bicycles.

Regulations: No dogs; no camping; observe warning signs on abandoned buildings.

Phone: 435-1915.

DESCRIPTION

There are two ways to explore the island: by going around it or by

Bicycling on Angel Island is a favorite family pastime

The deer of Angel Island are so tame they graze the lawn at Ayala Cove

Asian immigrants, below, in the late 1800's entered the U.S. through Angel Island's North Garrison, the "Ellis Island of the West." Detained on the quarantine ship, top; their belongings fumigated, above left; their quarters were far inferior to those of the army, above right (PHOTOS, COURTESY GGNRA)

climbing to the top of it. The trip around the island on old Army roads is about 6 miles long and takes in most of the historic sites. This level route is popular with bicyclists and also accommodates the elephant trains. The trip to the summit can be about 3 miles long or as much longer as you want, and is especially good for views and for studying the island's natural history. Actually, if you arrive fairly early in the day you can hike both routes, as described below.

No matter where you plan to go on the island, you will want to start at headquarters, a handsome white building overlooking Ayala Cove. The park staff is currently giving visitors a leaflet that tells a great deal about the island's history and contains a detailed trail map.

Most first-time visitors to the island make for Camp Reynolds on the western slope. Established in 1863, it was the first Army installation on the island. As we noted in the previous chapter, Alcatraz and Angel islands were to form the inner defense of the Bay against any invader who might

get through the Golden Gate. Continuing counterclockwise around the island, you can see where bigger guns were placed at the turn of the century at Battery Ledyard.

As you continue to walk counterclockwise around the south part of the island, you will have magnificent views of the City. On the southeast corner is Point Blunt, now a Coast Guard station but in the mid-19th century a favorite dueling ground for San Franciscans. Now, curving north, you come to the East Garrison, constructed during the Spanish-American War. This is the most extensively built-up portion of the island, and one alternative plan calls for it to become the major visitor center, perhaps including overnight camping facilities.

The North Garrison, much of which is currently off limits, was "the Ellis Island of the West" from 1910 to 1941. Many Asian immigrants were detained here for months, even years, under harsh and degrading conditions. Some of them bore witness to their bad treatment by writing poems on the walls, which remain today and are

The sheltered beach of Angel Island's East Garrison

remarkably moving. One plan for the island calls for restoring these detention barracks as a museum and preserving the poetic graffiti.

Soon after rounding Point Campbell, the northernmost part of the island, you come to the North Ridge Trail switchbacking up the bank to your left, across from a trail that runs back to the dock. It's about a mile up North Ridge to the summit, Mt. Caroline Livermore (781'), named for a Marin County conservationist who played a prominent role in having the island made a state park. You will note as you climb that there are fewer exotic plants like palm trees on the upper slopes of the island than there are below. Coast live oaks predominate along the trail, accompanied by buckeye and madrone. In spring, wildflowers run riot on the island, especially the higher portions— the result of seeding from airplanes.

On the North Ridge Trail just below its crossing of a fire road, the rangers in 1977 fenced off some young ceanothus, chamise and oak shrubs to assess the damage that deer were inflicting on the surrounding, unprotected shrubs. It turned out to be considerable. The deer of Angel Island had been much in the news for months: the herd had undergone a population explosion to perhaps 250 and were exhausting the small island's natural food supply. Not only were the deer themselves suffering from malnutrition and starvation, but also they were severely damaging the native plants by overbrowsing—and the plants are as much a part of the ecosystem the park is supposed to preserve as the animals are. As a short-term palliative, the San Francisco SPCA brought over several thousand pounds of hay to get the deer through the winter. Obviously, however, a more permanent solution is necessary. Some scientific-minded persons have suggested reintroducing on the island some of the deer's natural predators, such as

coyotes or mountain lions. While this program might make sense ecologically, it is probably not feasible politically: many city-dwellers would be afraid to visit a small island known to be inhabited by large, nonhuman predators. Furthermore, there would also be the possibility that a mountain lion might get bored with the island and might swim across Raccoon Strait to cause consternation on the tourist-crowded streets of Tiburon. The deer problem will probably be "solved" by moving most or even all of the herd to some wilder part of the state.

The North Ridge Trail continues up to the summit through pleasant oak forest. From the top you can enjoy a 360-degree view around the Bay. The most direct way back to Ayala Cove is by the Sunset Trail heading west. This trail descends fairly steeply through coastal scrub to Point Ione. The point itself is currently off limits because of erosion hazard, but a trail leads from here through the picnic area to the cove.

Walking around Angel Island; Tiburon and the old Northwestern Pacific depot are just across Raccoon Strait

MARIN HEADLANDS

Chapters 12 through 18

The almost pristine headlands on the north side of the Golden Gate are the heart of the GGNRA. After occupation by the military for almost a century, the availability at the right time of a large part of this area was a key factor in the establishment of the GGNRA.

T he first human inhabitants of the headlands area were the Coast Miwok Indians. In 1817 the Spanish established their first permanent settlement in the county, Mission San Rafael—partly for religious reasons, partly to serve as a buffer against the Russians to the north, operating out of Fort Ross. The padres resettled Indians from all over Marin County at the mission, and brought sick ones over from Mission Dolores in San Francisco, which was believed to be less salubrious. When the Mexican government secularized the missions in 1834, the Indians were either left to fend for themselves or

Looking down on Battery Spencer, once guardian of the Golden Gate, from Wolfback Ridge

forced into serfdom by the colonizers. Starvation and the white man's diseases soon killed them off.

Most of the headlands were part of Rancho Saucelito ("little grove of willows"), a spread of almost 20,000 acres which the Mexican government granted to William A. Richardson in 1838. Richardson, an English seaman, arrived in Yerba Buena (now San Francisco) on a whaler in 1822 under circumstances that remain obscure. Clyde F. Trudell, in *Old Marin with Love,* remarks drily: "A good deal has been written about Richardson and no doubt quite a bit of it is true. . .Some say he jumped ship at Yerba Buena; others that, having fought with his skipper, he was summarily put ashore; still others that, sobering up

Cormorants on rock near Tennessee Cove

White-crowned sparrow near the Miwok Trail

from a drunk ashore, he found his ship had sailed without him. A more romantic account credits his remaining to the charms of the sixteen-year-old daughter of the San Francisco Presidio Commandante." In any event, Richardson married that lady and in 1835 became the first Captain of the Port of San Francisco. After receiving his land grant, he moved to Marin County. From his headquarters at what is now Sausalito he sold beef, hides and produce—plus spring water at 50 cents per bucket—to sailing vessels and the young City. In Richardson's day, the valleys of Rancho Saucelito teemed with wildlife: bears, wolves, elk and mountain lions, in addition to the black-tailed deer that are still here.

The advent of the Civil War aroused apprehension that San Francisco Bay might be invaded by warships of the Confederacy, or some other hostile power, and, as we have seen, Alcatraz and Angel Island were fortified to defend the harbor. As larger guns with longer ranges were developed, it seemed desirable to fortify the Marin Headlands also, and in 1866 the Government purchased nearly 1900 acres overlooking the Bay. Originally called Lime Point Military Reservation, it was subse-

quently split into three posts named for commanding officers: Fort Baker (1897), Fort Barry (1904) and Fort Cronkhite (1937). The forts housed batteries of ever-more-sophisticated coastal artillery and, during World War II, antiaircraft guns. In the 1950s Nike missiles were installed; the last one was removed in 1974. Now that, in an era of intercontinental ballistic missiles, the forts can no longer serve as guardians of the Golden Gate, they have become part of the GGNRA, although some military personnel remain.

While the Army was occupying the southern headlands, the hills and valleys to the north continued as cattle ranches. After the construction of the Golden Gate Bridge and then World War II brought rapid population growth to Marin, it was inevitable that developers would seek to build on this land, so conveniently close to San Francisco. And sure enough, in 1964 an Eastern developer backed by the Gulf Oil Corporation proposed building Marincello, a "planned community" for 20,000 people on 2138 acres of the headlands. Alarmed conservationists fought the proposal for years, and in 1972 Gulf finally sold the land to The Nature Conservancy, which subsequently turned

Coast defense gun tube being hauled up 6% grade near Waldo Summit, August, 1939
(PHOTO, COURTESY GGNRA)

it over to the GGNRA. The land proposed for Marincello was rechristened the Martha Alexander Gerbode Preserve, in honor of a leading San Francisco environmentalist.

As a look at the topo map—or a climb to the top of a hill—will show, the headlands section of the GGNRA consists mainly of southeast-northwest trending open ridges separated by watercourses. Vigorous hikers can see quite a bit of the country in one day by going up and down the ridges on the Pacific Coast or the Miwok Trail. For example, it is only 5.8 miles (9.4 km) from Rodeo Cove to Muir Beach via the Pacific Coast Trail. Admittedly, this route has some steep climbs, but a strong hiker can manage it in a day. However, until the GGNRA establishes an intrapark transit system or a series of hostels, you will have to arrange a two-car shuttle for almost any extended one-way hike.

More leisurely hikers may wish to stroll along the protected valleys, each

Battery Wagner, constructed 1899-1901

The rugged Marin coast

Slide Ranch, 30-40 men's.
    Pt. Reyes 556-0560

Hwy 1 to Muir Beach
    2 miles beyond
    on left dirt road
        toward ocean
    yellow post —
        if chained go
        beyond 1/4 mile
        to next dirt road.
    park, walk
        down.

                    meet Howard Johnson

Boynton

page (a) set 1 & 2
(a2) A 1-9

San Francisco and the Bay Bridge viewed from Wolfback Ridge

of which eventually leads to a sheltered beach.

The outings described in the following pages are just a sample of the rambles possible in the headlands. With the aid of the *Trail Guide* mentioned above and a pair of good Vibram-soled boots you can explore at your will.Even without a map, you can't get seriously lost here, because if in doubt you can always climb to the top of one of the treeless hills and orient yourself.

MAPS: Topo *Point Bonita* and *San Francisco North; Trail Guide* published by the Coastal Parks Association available at ranger station ($.25); "Detailed Map of the Marin Peninsula" inset in the C.E. Erickson *Recreational Map: Golden Gate National Recreation Area* ($1.25).

Most of the "trails" in the Marin sections of the GGNRA are old Army or ranch roads. The topos show nearly all such roads, including the ones that are not official GGNRA trails; the

Erickson map shows most of them; the Coastal Parks Association's "Trail Guide" shows mainly the official trails, the military installations and the access roads. The maps in this book do not show all the old roads leading off from the routes described.

Facilities: Ranger station at Building 1050, Rodeo Beach (phone 561-7612) provides visitor information, parking, water, restrooms, phone; group camping by reservation only; hang gliding permitted in designated section of Rodeo Valley after checking in with ranger station.

Regulations: No trailbikes; no motorized vehicles; no smoking on trails; no guns; no dogs on trails; dogs permitted on Rodeo and Muir beaches subject to regulations; swimming not advised; observe caution when exploring old bunkers; stay well away from hazardous cliffs; in the back country, always close cattle gates after you; on riding-hiking trails, give equestrians the right of way.

12. Rodeo Beach

HOW TO GET THERE

BY BUS: During the summers of 1975 and 1976, San Francisco's Muni ran weekend buses to this section of the headlands, thus making it accessible to thousands of City dwellers. But in spring of 1977 neither the Muni nor the National Park Service would commit itself to funding such buses for another summer.

BY CAR: From Highway 101 northbound take the Alexander Avenue exit (the first one after Vista Point), pass the tunnel leading back to San Francisco, and immediately turn left at the signs for Forts Barry and Cronkhite. From 101 southbound, take the Sausalito exit, curve back under the freeway and immediately turn left at the sign for the forts. You will confront a one-way, half-mile-long tunnel for which a light regulates traffic. Once through the tunnel, continue along Bunker Road to Rodeo Lagoon, the beach and the ranger station.

FEATURES

The park service sponsors free walks in the Marin headlands area every weekend. They are led by enthusiastic rangers who do their best to answer questions— anything from "What would happen if I ate a planarian?" to "What will this beach look like a million years from now?" In general, the walks are oriented toward the study of the area's ecology, but they may also include Miwok indian culture or San Francisco's coastal defense system if participants are interested. To find out what is scheduled,

Beachcombing on Rodeo Beach in front of Bird Island

phone the ranger station. Organized groups can also arrange special walking tours by phoning two or three weeks in advance.

Facilities: Visitor information center, water, restrooms, phones, fire rings in the sand, lots of parking; hang gliding permitted in a designated area—ask the ranger station for the rules.

Regulations: Rodeo Beach is one of two portions of the GGNRA in Marin where dogs are allowed to run free. Dogs may run on South Rodeo Beach 24 hours a day and on North Rodeo Beach from 6:30 p.m. to 9:30 a.m., if they are within sight and voice control of the owner; during the day they must be on leash on North Rodeo Beach. Dogs are *not* allowed on any of the hiking trails. Swimming is hazardous and inadvisable.

Phone: 561-7612

Marin headlands ranger station (by tree) at Rodeo Lagoon, in front of old Army barracks

DESCRIPTION

Begin your visit at the ranger station, a converted Army building. Here you can pick up maps of the headlands and browse in the small natural-history museum. The best way to get acquainted with the area is to take one of the free guided walks, but if your schedule doesn't permit that, there are plenty of things to explore on your own.

Mallards in Rodeo Lagoon

Ranger leading a nature walk into the brush at Fort Cronkhite

Rodeo Lagoon (named for the cattle round-ups William A. Richardson held in the valley when he owned Rancho Saucelito) is never quite the same from season to season. The beach usually blocks Rodeo Creek from the sea, and the creek's fresh (albeit sometimes polluted) water backs up to form the lagoon—until a storm breaks the sand barrier and the ocean comes rushing in.

The beach is a joy for rockhounds because its multicolored pebbles include jasper, carnelian, agate and other semiprecious stones. Anglers can try their luck for surfperch from beach or rocks. Birders can stroll south to guano-covered Bird Island to watch cormorants and brown pelicans, and at low tide can make their way to a small beach just beyond it. (But watch out: this is one of those beaches where you can get trapped

LEGEND

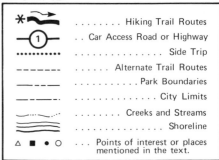

.... Hiking Trail Routes
.. Car Access Road or Highway
.... Side Trip
...... Alternate Trail Routes
.... Park Boundaries
.... City Limits
.... Creeks and Streams
.... Shoreline
... Points of interest or places mentioned in the text.

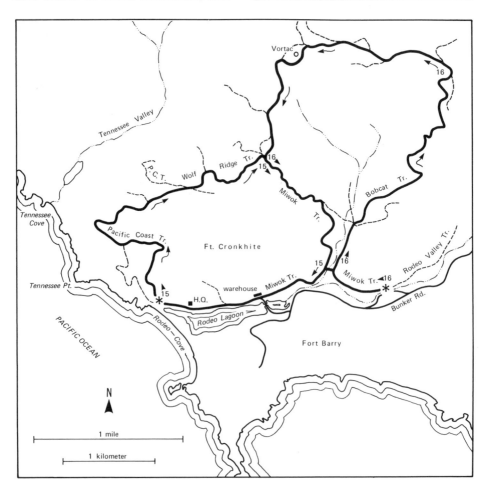

if you don't keep your eye on the incoming tide.)

On a hill behind the ranger station, in an old Nike Missile Site, is the California Marine Mammal Rehabilitation Center. This is not, as it might at first sound, a juvenile home for delinquent porpoises, but rather a sort of veterinary hospital where sick and wounded seals and sea lions from up and down the coast are tended until they are well enough to be restored to a suitable beach. The center is open to the public, and tours can be arranged for groups; phone 561-7284.

Looking down on Bird Island from an abandoned Army structure at Fort Cronkhite

13. Kirby Cove

HOW TO GET THERE

BY CAR: From Highway 101 north-bound, cross the Golden Gate Bridge and take the Alexander Avenue exit; immediately turn left (where the sign shows the route back to San Francisco) and at the first fork bear right, uphill, on unsigned Conzelman Road, fol-lowing the signs for forts Baker, Barry and Cronkhite. From Highway 101 southbound, take the Sausalito exit, turn left and then immediately turn right, following the signs for the forts. A short half mile from the freeway find a parking area on your left by an old brick Army structure. From here it's a walk of a bit over a mile down a graveled road to the cove.

FEATURES

When you look north from San Fran-cisco's beaches and headlands, you can see an oasis of dark green trees punctu-ating the otherwise barren Marin cliffs. They are the eucalyptus, Monterey pine and Monterey cypress of Kirby Cove. These three kinds of tree are just as foreign to Marin County as they originally were to San Francisco, where, as we have seen, they were extensively introduced in the 19th Century. The grove at Kirby Cove was planted before World War I by a soldier then stationed at Fort Barry, William Dillon, the father of author Richard H. Dillon.

For anyone who is willing to walk an easy three-mile round trip, Kirby Cove offers a protected picnic spot with spectacular views of the Bay and the City. (The trip down and back can be unexpectedly windy, so bring an extra sweater.) The cove also contains one of the few group camping sites in the GGNRA.

Facilities: Water, privies, picnic tables, grills; group camping by reservation (phone 561-7612).

Looking at the City from the often-deserted beach at Kirby Cove

Regulations: No pets; swimming highly inadvisable. Additional regulations for camping groups may be obtained from the Park Service.

DESCRIPTION

The mile-long walk down to the cove is enlivened by the ever-changing views of the Golden Gate Bridge, downtown San Francisco, the Presidio, the omnipresent Sutro Tower, Bakers Beach, Seacliff, Phelan Beach, Lincoln Park, Mile Rock Light and, of course, whatever ships happen to be passing through the Golden Gate. You pass above Battery Wagner's two gun emplacements and get a brief glimpse of Point Diablo below you to the west. If the panorama should pall, you can study the plants on the bank to your right: lots of fennel and California sagebrush, and in spring a surprising number of colorful wildflowers—poppies, lupine, paintbrush, monkey flower, morning

Battery Kirby, constructed 1898-1900

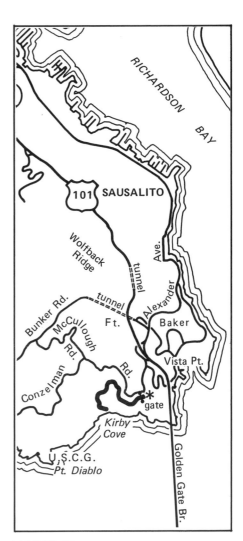

LEGEND

✳🔛	. . . . Hiking Trail Routes
—①—	. . Car Access Road or Highway
••••••••••	. . . . Side Trip
— — — —	. . . . Alternate Trail Routes
——————	. . . . Park Boundaries
— — —•—	. . . . City Limits
〰〰〰	. . . . Creeks and Streams
〰〰〰	. . . . Shoreline
△ ■ ● ○	. . . Points of interest or places mentioned in the text.

Our state flower, the California poppy (Eschscholzia californica)

glory, phacelia and buckwheat. An abundant, shrubby, white-flowered plant is a member of the eupatory tribe that has immigrated to the Marin headlands from Mexico. Sections of the dark red chert bank are layered and tilted in amazingly picturesque fashion.

The road ends in the grove. From here you can follow trails past the picnicking and camping areas to the narrow beach. At low tide you can explore the caves of fantastically twisted red-brown-purple chert at the east end of the cove. Toward the west end of the beach, a low brick tunnel leads to Battery Kirby. Like Battery Wagner above, it dates from the turn of the century and originally held two guns, each with a range of 12 miles.

From the beach you can get a Bay-level view of the maritime traffic that goes through the Golden Gate every day: sailboats, fishing craft, tankers, freighters, ungainly container ships and an occasional passenger liner calculated to bring wanderlust to the heart of the beachcombing picnicker. Perhaps Kirby Cove conveys as well as any place the feature that makes the GGNRA unique—the juxtaposition of a great city and a natural, semi-wild place. Picnicking, fishing or sunbathing on the beach, you can see San Francisco's

Huge Monterey cypress at Kirby Cove

skyline spread out before you, and the Golden Gate Bridge less than a mile away, but the muted hum from the bridge's traffic is almost drowned out by the splash of waves lapping the shore at your feet.

SIDE TRIP

For yet another great view of the Golden Gate, walk out to Battery Spencer, near the parking place.

14. Exploring Forts Baker and Barry

HOW TO GET THERE

BY CAR: From Highway 101 north-bound, cross the Golden Gate Bridge and take the Alexander Avenue exit; immediately turn left (where the sign shows the route back to San Francisco) and at the first fork bear right, uphill, on unsigned Conzelman Road, fol-lowing the signs for forts Baker, Barry and Cronkhite. From Highway 101 southbound, take the Sausalito exit, turn left and then immediately turn right, following the signs for the forts.

FEATURES

The old forts overlooking the Golden Gate are a spectacular place to bring out-of-town visitors for a picnic, or just an hour's drive. The views are un-paralleled, and the defunct batteries provide an eerie historical note.

This is one of the few parts of the GGNRA which I recommend recon-noitering by car before you tackle it on foot. There are plenty of trails and old roads here that are off-limits to mo-torized vehicles; you can scout them

Fort Baker's Battery Wagner defended the Golden Gate

from your car and decide which ones you want to explore more fully.

If you are a fairly strong cyclist, you can bicycle across the Golden Gate Bridge and follow the signed bike routes around the forts.

Facilities: No water; privies at Hill 129; a few picnic tables near Battery Wallace.

Regulations: Observe cautionary signs on old bunkers and eroding cliffs.

DESCRIPTION

Conzelman Road runs uphill past Battery Spencer and the entrance to Kirby Cove and, just over a mile from Highway 101, reaches a junction with McCullough Road. The Pacific Coast Trail for riders and hikers leads west from this intersection at a gate signed *Fire lane.* The eastward continuation of the Pacific Coast Trail is a few hundred feet north of the intersection at a riding-hiking trail sign. This portion of the trail runs up the red ridge above Rodeo Valley toward Wolfback Ridge.

Continuing to drive up Conzelman Road, you soon come to a parking area for Hill 129. Here is the largest and most recent of the forts' batteries. By the time Battery Hill 129 (the only one *not* named after a soldier) was completed in 1944, "the gun it was to hold had already become obsolete, so it was

Inside an old bunker at Fort Barry

Battery Hill 129, constructed during World War II

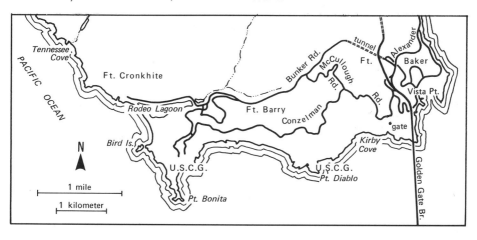

Coast Guard housing at Point Bonita; Battery Hill 129 (with trees) in the distance

never used," according to Teresa M. Fenn in *Old Marin With Love.* We have seen similar examples of instant military obsolescence both before and after the building of Battery Hill 129, and no doubt will continue to see more.

You can still see the huge circular hole for the gun emplacement on the west side of the battery. The entire subterranean structure is awesome in size and massiveness—and no doubt was in expense, too.

From Hill 129 Conzelman Road continues west as a one-way route along the cliff, always overlooking the spectacular view of the Golden Gate. The road is graveled for a stretch. Eventually it loops around another large installation, Battery Wallace, completed in 1942. The battery is "camouflaged" by a grove of Monterey cypress planted over it. Since this is by far the largest grove of trees on the otherwise nearly

bare hills, it must be remarkably conspicuous to any aircraft flying over the headlands. Fortunately, Japanese bombers never reached Fort Barry.

A few picnic tables are located near the battery. If you walk south along the sandy paths that lead to the promontories overlooking the Golden Gate, you may see a few really determined sunbathers who have—despite the park's warning signs—ventured down the steep cliffs to pockets of beach. Or you can drive to the westernmost parking area and walk to the observation platform that overlooks Bird Island and the ruggedly majestic coast.

The Coast Guard occupies the Point Bonita peninsula. The first light at Point Bonita was installed in 1855. It was 324 feet above the water and was frequently obscured by high fogs. In 1877 the light was moved 200 feet down to its present location on a rapidly eroding promontory. Until a few years ago it was possible to visit the lighthouse by going through a low rock tunnel and across a narrow, swaying suspension bridge—a journey calculated to strike terror into the hearts of both claustrophobes and acrophobes. The Coast Guard judged the trip too hazardous for the increasing numbers of visitors, and now the lighthouse and its approaches are definitely *off limits* to the public, as indicated by prominent signs.

You cannot retrace your route on one-way Conzelman Road, so you must return to Highway 101 via Rodeo Valley and either Bunker Road through the tunnel or McCullough Road back up to Conzelman. Or you can finish your excursion with a visit to Rodeo Beach (see Chapter 12).

West end of the Bunker Road tunnel leading from Fort Baker to forts Barry and Cronkhite

An abandoned Army observation post at Fort Cronkhite

15. Wolf Ridge Loop

HOW TO GET THERE
See Chapter 12

FEATURES
This loop trip of about 5 miles (8 km) is a great introduction to the headlands, because it includes some of this terrain's most distinctive features: rolling, treeless ridges that offer ever-changing views up and down the coast and over adjacent valleys; occasional abandoned fortifications, many of them situated on hilltops like medieval castles; and a feeling of wildness and solitude that is almost incredible only four miles from San Francisco as the cormorant flies.

Another characteristic feature of the headlands is windiness. Bring a jacket!

Facilities: Water, restrooms, at Rodeo Beach ranger station; none along the trail.

Regulations: No pets, no fires.

DESCRIPTION
From the parking lot north of the old Army barracks at Rodeo Beach, find the Pacific Coast Trail sign, which shows distances to various points and indicates by symbols that the trail is usable by hikers and equestrians. As the trail ascends gently over the exposed hill, the sound of the ocean behind you gradually recedes. The most conspicuous vegetation along this portion of the trail is coyote brush (*Baccharis pilularis* variety *consanguinea*), a shrub that is extremely common along the northern California coast. It is a dioecious species, meaning that all the flowers on any one plant are of a single sex. (In most species, every flower has both stamens, which are male parts, and pistils, which are female parts.) If you hike here in fall, when the female plants are flowering, you can easily see why this shrub is also called "fuzzy-wuzzy." An occasional introduced

Walking past coyote brush on the Pacific Coast Trail

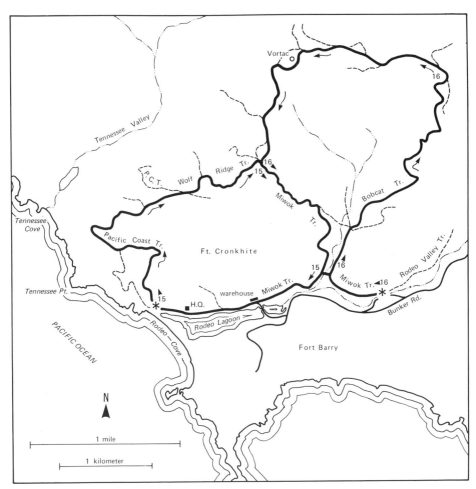

N

1 mile

1 kilometer

exotic plant (e.g., acacia, pampas grass) lends variety to the vegetative scene.

When the trail joins a paved road, go left (west) on it. At a saddle another paved road goes left toward Battery Townsley. Pause here to look back and enjoy the view: part of Rodeo Lagoon, Bird Island, a glimpse of Point Bonita lighthouse, and the City in the distance (where, as usual, Sutro Tower dominates the scene).

Continue west on the paved Pacific Coast Trail. When it makes a broad switchback, you can look northwest to see Tennessee Cove and the Muir Beach headlands with their eccentric architecture. As the trail continues gradually ascending Wolf Ridge (passing some mouldering military installations) you have views of the Golden Gate Bridge, more of the City, and eventually the

Tennessee Cove viewed from Wolf Ridge

three peaks of Mt. Tamalpais. An intriguing white object that looks like a monument, on a hilltop to the east, is a prominent landmark for hikers on these headlands trails. This is a Federal Aviation Administration installation, official called a Very High Frequency Omni-Range and Tactical Air Navigation Aid—familiarly referred to as Vortac. It is a long-distance directional homing device for commercial aircraft.

When a sign on the left shows the junction of the Pacific Coast and Wolf Ridge trails, scramble off the road (which continues to a deactivated Nike station) and begin descending on the Wolf Ridge Trail. Far below on your left is pastoral Tennessee Valley, in which you will probably see cows

grazing. This valley was to be the grand entrance to the ill-fated Marincello project, which was intended to cover with tract houses and highrises much of the land that spreads before you.

The trail contours around a steep cliff of layered red chert under the former Nike base, then runs east along a barbed wire fence. When you come to a green gate, go through it (closing it behind you). This is a good spot to lunch, look for hawks and vultures, and enjoy the view before you start descending. (Determined hikers who want to go on for about another 4 miles, or 6½ km., can continue uphill here and return by way of the Bobcat Trail, described in the next chapter.)

To return to Rodeo Valley, descend

on the Miwok Trail. On your right is a hillside which is ablaze with poppies in spring; on your left a willow-bordered creek, which is home to goldfinches and other birdlife (see next chapter) and eventually the remains of the old Silva ranch house. Ahead of you are the Fort Barry stables. The Silva family were among Marin's most prominent citizens of Portuguese descent. They owned ranches in western Marin, as well as the 2200-acre one here that almost became Marincello.

When you reach a trail junction, bear right and cross the meadow to the big white warehouse. The most scenic way back is on the lagoon side of Bunker Road. Here you will invariably see birds (who don't mind the water pollution)—egrets, great blue herons and assorted ducks.

A common egret in Rodeo Lagoon

A young buck black-tailed deer with antlers in velvet

16. A Bobcat Trail/Miwok Trail Loop

HOW TO GET THERE

BY CAR: Take the Alexander Avenue exit and go through the tunnel, as described in Ch. 12. A mile from the end of the tunnel, a road goes off to the right in an arc. Near the center of the arc a sign announces the Miwok Trail. You can park on the roadside.

FEATURES

This is a wonderful hike for a spring day because of the profusion of wildflowers along the way during springtime. Birders also will find much to intrigue them. The total distance is about 5 miles, or 8 km; the first half is mostly uphill, but not steeply.

Facilities: None; bring water and lunch.

Regulations: No pets, no fires.

DESCRIPTION

The Miwok Trail begins as a footbridge crossing a creek bordered by willows—the only trees native to this part of the headlands. Once across the creek, bear left on an old farm road that runs through a meadow. You may see both Brewer's and red-winged blackbirds here, and quite possibly a red-tailed hawk or a marsh hawk. The path soon runs into a trail junction at another creek. Turn right here on the Bobcat Trail (unsigned at present), which runs above the east bank of this creek. Birders should pause to study the willows and shrubbery in the creek, which are a haunt of goldfinches. With luck and patience you may also see a northern (formerly Bullock's) oriole or a lazuli bunting, a species in which the male has upper parts of bright

Hang gliders wait for wind on the Miwok Trail above the remains of the Silva Ranch buildings

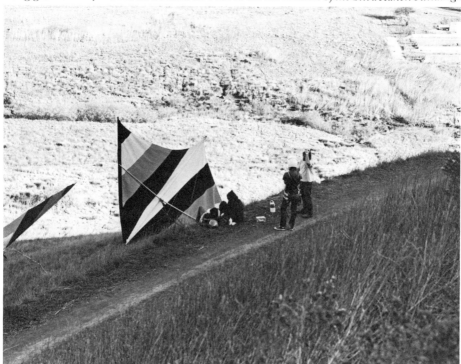

Looking from Wolfback Ridge over the Bay to the Presidio, Golden Gate Park, the University of California Medical Center and Mount Sutro

Filaree, a native of the Old World that has become common in Marin County

The iris is one of the most beautiful native spring wildflowers

turquoise (the female, however, is described by Roger Tory Peterson as "nondescript").

The trail ascends gently past the foundations of the old Silva ranch house. There are several introduced trees here—most conspicuously a stand of eucalyptus. The thistle, radish and mustard you have been walking through are not native plants either; but the poppy and lupine on the hillside are, as is the coastal scrub (coyote brush, California sagebrush) that borders the trail. As you continue to climb gradually, you come upon more and more wildflowers: paintbrush, morning glory, monkey flower, wild cucumber, checker bloom, blue-eyed grass, yarrow, narrow-leaved mule ears, iris and, in the moister places, columbine. The view back over the lagoon, Fort Barry and the ocean becomes increasingly panoramic.

As you near the crest of the hill, you go under a power line and pass a couple of roads coming in from the right. The trail curves west, and Mt. Tamalpais's three summits are visible to the north. You soon reach a barbed wire fence with a hiker's stile that gives access to a gray rock outcropping. It makes a good lunch spot because of its superb view of Richardson Bay, the Tiburon peninsula, and in clear weather a panorama stretching north as far as Mt. St. Helena.

After lunch, return to the Bobcat Trail by the stile or a break in the barbed wire. The trail descends briefly, then ascends steadily toward the rocket-like Vortac visible to the west. Pass a road on the right leading down to Tennessee Valley. As you climb, the view becomes ever more encompassing; you can see south to Ocean Beach and Point San Pedro, and east to Mt. Diablo. When you are almost at the summit of the Vortac's hill, you pass a sign showing where the Miwok Trail goes north, downhill to Tennessee Valley. To pick up the Miwok Trail going south, back to Rodeo Valley, you have to go clockwise around the Vortac's fence to the road going downhill to the southwest.

The trail descends, steeply in places, for about ½ mile to reach the junction with Wolf Ridge Trail at a green gate. The rest of the descent is as described in the latter part of the preceding chapter, until you reach the valley floor: there, of course, you bear left, across the creek, rather than right, toward the warehouse.

17. Tennessee Valley

HOW TO GET THERE

BY BUS: GGT #10 and #20 stop at Shoreline Highway and Tennessee Valley Road (near Le Camembert Restaurant), about 1½ miles from the trailhead.
BY CAR: From Highway 101 take the Stinson Beach exit to Shoreline Highway (Highway 1); less than a half mile from 101 find Tennessee Valley Road running southwest and follow it to the parking lot.

FEATURES

For many years this lush valley was part of the Witter Ranch and definitely off-limits to hikers. In 1976 its 1268 acres became an extremely welcome addition to the GGNRA. The comfortable, mostly level trail that leads for about 2 miles (3 km) to a small, protected beach is suitable for young and old, and even for bicycles.

Facilities: No water; privies at trailhead and near beach.

Regulations: No vehicles, no dogs, no fires, swimming hazardous and highly inadvisable; obey signs warning against climbing eroding cliffs at the beach.

DESCRIPTION

The trail begins at the red-tiled, pseudo-mission-style entrance gates that are among the few remnants of the gran-

Looking north from the Miwok Trail over Tennessee Valley

diose Marincello project discussed earlier. Note the Miwok Trail running north and south from the Tennessee Valley trailhead; from strolling the various valleys in the headlands you can get a good idea of whether you'd like to take the Miwok (or, farther on, the Pacific Coast) Trail over the hills. The Tennessee Valley Trail begins as a paved road, but it has footpaths on either side for walkers who don't like paving. The route gradually descends along a small creek bordered by eucalyptus trees. As you stroll through this bucolic valley, you will probably see horses, which the Park Service raises for the rangers, and cattle. If you had been here in the days when the valley was part

of William A. Richardson's Rancho Saucelito, you would have seen some wilder animals. Charles Lauff, one of Richardson's guests during Christmas of 1847, describes a bear hunt in nearby Rodeo Valley, at which not only a bear but also a mountain lion was captured, and adds: "As we passed into the Tennessee Valley, the hillside was white with bones of elk, deer and wild coyote killed from time to time for their hides." The hunting tradition continued into the 20th Century in the form of a gun club on the Witter Ranch.

You pass a mission-style house and some farm buildings on your left *(private)* and a bike rack on your right, and continue to descend gradually on

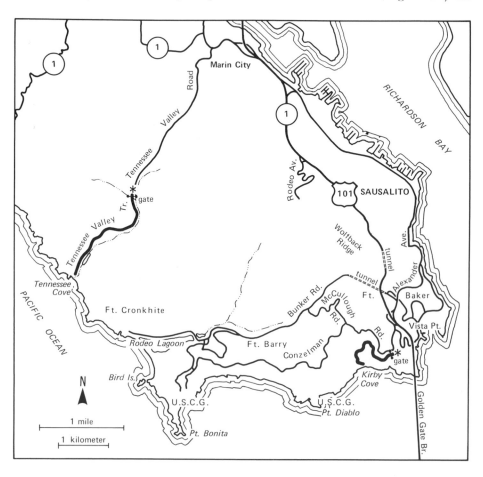

the trail, which is now a graveled road, along the willow-lined creek. At a fork bear left, where a sign shows the continuation of the trail over a meadow. (The graveled road—more suitable for bicycles—goes past the former gun club and subsequently rejoins the main trail.) Soon after crossing a tributary creek on a culvert, you pass the intersection with the Pacific Coast Trail. Now the Tennessee Valley Trail forks: the Park Service has christened the left branch the Wok Mi Trail! It crosses the creek on a footbridge and curves around the south bank of the mallard-frequented lagoon. In spring there are wildflowers here: poppies, lupines, wild cucumbers, baby-blue-eyes and buttercups; at any time of year there is *poison oak,* which you can

Hikers should always close cattle gates behind them

The end of the trail: the beach at Tennessee Cove

LEGEND

✳ 〜	. . . . Hiking Trail Routes
—①—	. . Car Access Road or Highway
••••••••••	. . . . Side Trip
– – – – –	. . . . . . Alternate Trail Routes
—— ——	. . . . Park Boundaries
—— — —.	. . . . City Limits
⌣‿⌣	. . . . Creeks and Streams
≈≈≈	. . . . Shoreline
△ ■ • ○	. . . Points of interest or places mentioned in the text.

Sailing past Tennessee Point

Trails run around both sides of Tennessee Valley Lagoon

easily avoid if you keep your eyes open.

The Wok Mi Trail circles back to the main trail along the earthen weir that dams Tennessee Creek to form a lagoon. From here it's a short walk to the beach guarded by steep cliffs. Even if it's a windy day, you can probably find a sheltered spot to stretch out, picnic and watch the cormorants on the rugged seastacks offshore. If you hear the fog-buoy mooing like a wounded seacow, you might try to visualize the terrifying event of March 6, 1853, which gave this cove, point and valley their name: On that foggy night the steamship *Tennessee,* carrying six hundred passengers, including a hundred women and children, missed the Golden Gate and went aground here. Fortunately all the passengers were saved, but the ship was wrecked. The next year, the Government constructed the first lighthouse on the Pacific Coast, on Alcatraz, and the year after that the first one in Marin County, on Point Bonita.

18. Muir Beach and Green Gulch

HOW TO GET THERE

BY BUS: As this book goes to press, GGT is running occasional buses (#61) to Muir Woods via Muir Beach on weekends and holidays. This service may vary seasonally, so check with GGT first.

BY CAR: From Highway 101 take the Stinson Beach exit to Shoreline Highway (Highway 1). At the junction with Panoramic Highway, bear left to continue on Shoreline. (Soon after this junction, note the Miwok Trail coming in from a eucalyptus grove on the left and running over a bare hill to the right.) Continue down Shoreline, passing the (private) entrance to the Wheelwright Green Gulch Zen Center on your left. When Shoreline levels off and turns north, find the Muir Beach Road

on your left opposite a long string of mailboxes. See map on page 116.

FEATURES

Muir Beach is larger and more accessible by auto than Tennessee Cove, but not nearly so large and crowded as

LEGEND

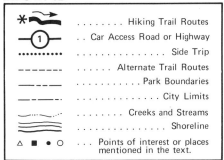

```
*  ⤳      . . . . . . . Hiking Trail Routes
─①─      . . Car Access Road or Highway
••••••••  . . . . . . . . . . . . . Side Trip
- - - - -  . . . . . . Alternate Trail Routes
─────    . . . . . . . . . . Park Boundaries
─ ·· ─ ·· ─  . . . . . . . . . . . City Limits
≈≈≈≈≈    . . . . . . . Creeks and Streams
〰〰〰    . . . . . . . . . . . . . Shoreline
△ ■ ● ○  . . . Points of interest or places
             mentioned in the text.
```

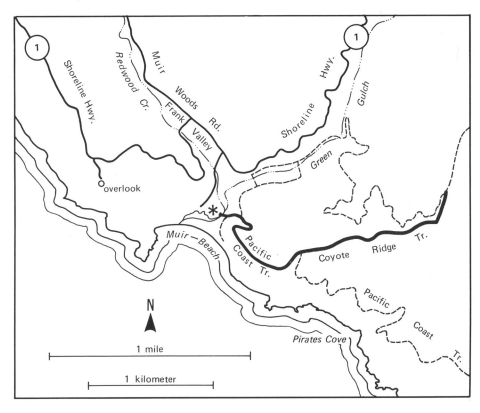

always-popular Stinson Beach to the north. Like all these coastal beaches, it can be windy, but you can usually find a sheltered spot for picnicking. You can spend a lazy day here with your lunch, your Frisbee or your book. On the other hand, if you want an exhilarating ramble, you can hike to the top of Coyote Ridge.

Facilities: Water, privies, picnic tables, phone.

Regulations: Dogs allowed on beach but not on trails or in the Zen Center.

DESCRIPTION

From the picnic area go southeast over a wooden bridge. The Redwood Creek that runs through Muir Woods flows to the ocean here. The maps show it forming Big Lagoon just inside a sandbar, but at this writing, after two years of drought, the lagoon is more like a marsh. Go through a green gate to reach the signed Pacific Coast Trail. At the junction with the trail leading to the Zen Center farm, go right, uphill.

As you climb, you can look over the lagoon (or marsh, or meadow, depending on climatic conditions) and see the idiosyncratic houses of Muir Beach Heights. Continuing up, in less than a mile (1.2 km) you reach the Coyote Ridge Trail.

A glance at the topo map or the Erickson map reveals that a number of old ranch roads wander in every direction from Coyote Ridge. Eventually some of them will be incorporated into the GGNRA's trail system. Meanwhile, you can hardly get lost, because you can see for miles over the rolling hills and over the ocean behind you. For a workout you might want to drop down to Pirates Cove or even as far as Tennessee Valley (2.2 miles, 3.5 km). For an easier trip, you can take one of the roads, or go cross-country, down to the Green Gulch Zen Center Farm—an oasis of vegetable garden nestled between the hills. If you visit the Zen Center, be sure to close the gates after you as requested, so that deer will not get at the crops.

Surf fishing off rocks near Muir Beach

Trail in Douglas fir grove beside the Muir Beach road

From Vista Point (right center) you can overlook Muir Beach and see south to San Francisco

SIDE TRIP

On Highway 1 a little over 1¼ miles north of Muir Beach a discreet sign *Vista Point* shows the road to Muir Beach Overlook, a mini-park (privies, picnic tables) on steep cliffs high above the ocean. A few gun emplacements still remain here from World War II. A narrow path with a handrail leads to the end of the promontory, whence one can look north to Point Reyes, east to the Farallon Islands, south to Point San Pedro, and down to the rugged seastacks along this wild coast. Another path leads south past a gun emplacement to a viewspot overlooking Muir Beach. Please *stay on the paths* (acrophobes will not need this warning), because the cliffs here are much given to slides.

MT. TAMALPAIS MUIR WOODS AND STINSON BEACH

Chapters 19 through 23

*These are among the most heavily used parks in the Bay region. To many Bay Areans, **hike** means Mt. Tamalpais and the forests and beaches at its feet. In fact, scores of people are content to hike there regularly and almost never go anywhere else.*

T he mountain's great popularity is due to its proximity to the metropolitan area, its magnificent views, its remarkably varied terrain and its long history of accessibility by public transit—including, for many years, "the Crookedest Railroad in the World." The tall trees of Muir Woods are a world-renowned tourist attraction. And the long, protected strand of Stinson

Beach has for more than a century been a magnet for urbanites who wanted to swim, fish and beachcomb.

Since Mt. Tamalpais, Muir Woods and Stinson Beach are contiguous with the GGNRA and share the same trails and access routes, it might seem logical for all these places to become part of the GGNRA; and geographically they are— but not politically. So far only Stinson Beach, previously a state park, has been transferred to the GGNRA. Muir Woods remains a national monument, a small enclave surrounded by state park. The

Fog rushes in through the Golden Gate as hikers approach the top of the Old Mine Trail on Mt. Tamalpais in the sunshine

north and west slopes of the mountain, which are watershed lands, remain under the control of the Marin Municipal Water District, which allows them to be used for recreational purposes.

Originally, Mt. Tamalpais State Park, which occupies the south and east flanks of the mountain, was scheduled to become part of the GGNRA. However, the dedicated stalwarts of the Tamalpais Conservation Club, which since its formation in 1912 has been protecting the mountain, lobbied against this plan. They argued that the state-park system was doing an excellent job of managing the area, and that a remote federal bureaucracy might seek to over-promote and overdevelop it (shades of Yosemite). They also invoked the mountain's guardian spirit, botanist Alice Eastwood, who said back in 1914: "I am not in sympathy with any movement to change Mt. Tamalpais. Its greatest charm is its individuality and its rugged wildness enhanced by proximity to a large city." The TCC and its

Hiking through Douglas firs on the old stage road on Mt. Tamalpais

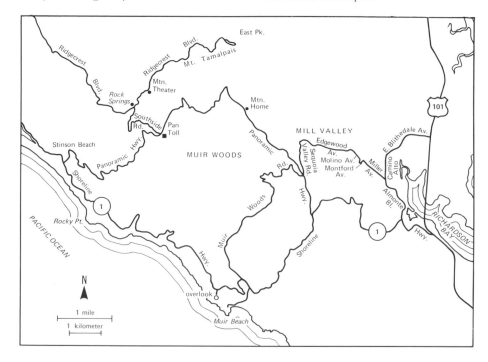

allies carried the day, so Mt. Tamalpais will remain a state park for the foreseeable future. However, it will be included in long-range planning for the GGNRA and Point Reyes National Seashore.

The Tamalpais area is unusually subject to fire. During the 19th Century, forest fires devoured thousands of acres of timber on the slopes of the mountain and Bolinas Ridge. A fire in 1913 destroyed Muir Inn, and one in 1923 the Tamalpais Tavern on East Peak. An even worse fire in 1929 burned more than a hundred houses in Mill Valley and virtually destroyed the Crookedest Railroad in the World. Another major fire in 1945 burned 18,000 acres in the Kent Lake area; the charred trees are still very much in evidence.

Weather conditions in the 1970s have contributed greatly to fire hazard on Tamalpais. An unusual snowfall during January 1974 felled many trees on the higher portions of the mountain and seriously damaged many more. As it was impossible to clear out all the off-trail debris, trunks and branches have remained scattered all around. As this book goes to press, two years of drought have rendered them tinder-dry.

The water district and the park service will close off the mountain whenever the fire hazard becomes extremely severe, and the GGNRA may follow suit on its lands too. If you are planning to hike in the area during periods of very dry, hot weather, phone the Marin Fire Department (488-0123) or the Marin Municipal Water District (924-4600) the afternoon before to find out if roads and trails have been closed.

In a previous book (*An Outdoor Guide to the San Francisco Bay Area*, Wilderness Press, 1976) I have discussed Mt. Tamalpais and environs in detail and outlined 17 hikes there. In this book I include 3 hikes that border on,

Fog creeps toward Angel Island while Panoramic Highway on Mt. Tamalpais remains in the sun

Redwoods and ferns on the Bootjack Trail in Muir Woods

pass through or lead to GGNRA land. All of them begin at the Pan Toll ranger station, which is park head-quarters and a weekend/holiday GGT bus stop. Chapters 22 and 23 describe Muir Woods and Stinson Beach.

MAPS: Topos *San Rafael, Bolinas* and *Point Bonita;* free trail map available from Pan Toll ranger station; leaflet *Historic Tours: Mt. Tamalpais State Park* with sketch maps available from ranger station for $.25; C.E. Erickson (formerly Harry Freese) *Trail Map of the Mt. Tamalpais Region* available from map and sporting-goods stores for $1.00.

Facilities: Water, restrooms, picnic tables and grills at both Pan Toll and nearby Bootjack; phone at Pan Toll; 18 walk-in tent campsites at Pan Toll on a first-come, first-served basis, about 100 yards from the parking lot. (Some of these facilities may not be available during periods of drought.)

Regulations: The standard state-park rules:

Pets must be on leash or housed at the campsite or in a vehicle; dogs over 5 months old must have license or other proof of current rabies inoculation; *no dogs on trails;* fee of $1 per dog per night.

No firearms.

Fires are allowed only in designated places, and you must bring your own fuel or buy it from the rangers; collecting wood is not allowed.

Overnight camping is $2; day use and parking, $1.50.

Phone: 388-2070

Looking down on Stinson Beach, Bolinas and Duxbury Reef from the slopes of Mt. Tamalpais

19. Steep Ravine

HOW TO GET THERE

BY BUS: GGT #63 (Stinson Beach Bolinas) to Pan Toll on weekends and holidays.

BY CAR: From Highway 101 go west onto Highway 1 at the Stinson Beach exit. After 3 winding miles, where Highway 1 continues to Stinson Beach turn right on Panoramic Highway and follow signs reading *Mt. Tamalpais*. After 1 mile, pass the Muir Woods Road—Mill Valley junction. Continuing to follow *Mt. Tamalpais* signs, arrive in about 4 miles at the Pan Toll ranger station on your left. The parking fee here is $1.50 per day.

FEATURES

Steep Ravine has unusually large redwoods for such a narrow canyon so near the ocean. The ravine was formed by Webb Creek, which has been eroding the mountainside for centuries in its rush to the sea.

The first non-Indian hiker in the ravine was probably Lieutenant Felipe de Goycoechea, who explored the area in 1793; he noted that his party descended toward the ocean "by a deep ravine of pine trees which was traversed with difficulty." The weary lieutenant apparently felt that when you've seen one conifer, you've seen them all.

Steep Ravine, like nearby Muir Woods, was a gift to the public from Congressman William Kent, who donated it to the state for a park in 1928, shortly before his death.

The creek-side trail down Steep Ravine is probably at its best during early spring, when the water cascades freely and trilliums abound. Much of the trail is very steep indeed, and occasionally requires descending on rough wooden ladders and slippery stone steps, so good boots are essential.

DESCRIPTION

From the south end of the Pan Toll parking lot find the signed Steep Ravine Trail. It switchbacks down through redwood, fir, bay and huckle-

Near the top of the Steep Ravine Trail

Negotiating the stairs near the bottom of Steep Ravine

Webb Creek flows down Steep Ravine through fern and maple

berry for ½ mile to Webb Creek. From here the trail descends along the creek, crossing it from time to time on footbridges. The splashing stream almost entirely drowns out noise from nearby Panoramic Highway.

The hiker occasionally clambers over and under fallen redwoods. As one might expect in such a narrow, moist canyon, ferns abound: not only the sword fern, commonly found with redwoods, but also five-finger fern, spreading wood fern, goldback fern, California polypody, and leather fern hanging from rocks and trees.

After 1½ miles of descent, the Steep Ravine Trail joins the Dipsea Trail, which comes over a footbridge from the left, and continues 50 yards downstream to a dam. From here you can cut the hike short by turning right and following the Dipsea Trail to Stinson Beach. Or you can walk another mile to wind-swept Rocky Point. To do this, follow Webb Creek to Highway 1, either by the rough trail that runs along its west bank or by the fire road that branches off from the Dipsea Trail 50 yards west of the dam. Cross the highway and descend the lupine-covered slope on a rather steep trail, which appears on some of the older maps as the Warm Spring Trail.

From here you can explore the Rocky Point area at your leisure by fire road or trail, enjoying meadows, ponds and rugged headlands. As at other spots on this part of the coast, the remains of a few gun emplacements linger from World War II. On the northwest side of the point are 14 small, rather Spartan cabins that were built about 40 years

Looking out over the Pacific from Rocky Point

ago. Looking at these small, plain buildings, one could hardly guess that their fate has generated almost as much of a brouhaha as that of San Francisco's City of Paris or Fitzhugh Building. When the state took over this property in 1960, several prominent Bay Areans had long-term leases on these cabins at remarkably low rents. After years of controversy in the state legislature, the leases were finally terminated and the cabins vacated. However, since then the question of what to do with them has continued to exercise the legislature, the California Coastal Commission, and many local conservationists, including the stalwarts of the Tamalpais Conservation Club. Should the cabins be kept and used as hostels or as part of an environmental educational center? Should they be totally razed and the

area restored as nearly as possible to its natural state? The editor of the TCC's newsletter has advocated a "compromise" position of tearing them down as far as the floorboards.

To the north of the cabins is a beach of sand, rocks and driftwood, to which Webb Creek cascades down through willows.

Leave the beach by the steep path to the south of Webb Creek and return to the highway by curving north on an old farm road. As you climb past large, lichen-covered rock formations and wind-stunted bay trees, you can enjoy a magnificent ocean view. If you walk here at dusk, you might see a great horned owl silhouetted on a rock above the trail, scanning the steep hillside below.

As you approach the highway you

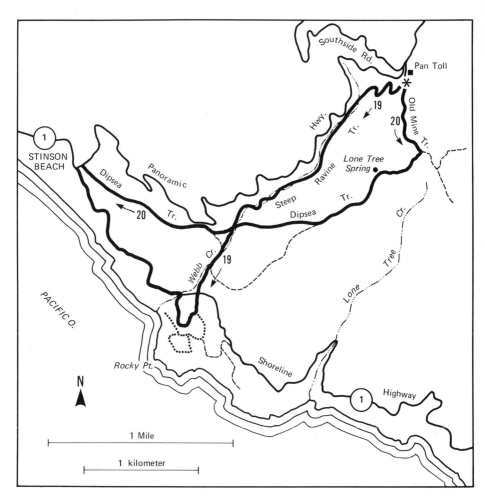

can hear Webb Creek rushing through alders and willows to your left. The old road ends at a locked gate and a small parking area just off Highway 1. From here you can walk 1 mile to Stinson Beach on the road's shoulder (a journey not recommended for small children); you can retrace your steps to the dam and hike the Dipsea Trail to Stinson Beach; or you can return to Pan Toll via either the Steep Ravine or the Dipsea Trail.

LEGEND

✳🌊➜	. . . . Hiking Trail Routes
―①―	. . Car Access Road or Highway
••••••••	. . . . Side Trip
– – – –	. . . . . . Alternate Trail Routes
— ——	. . . . Park Boundaries
— ——.	. . . . City Limits
—·—··—··	. . . . Creeks and Streams
〰〰〰	. . . . Shoreline
△ ■ ● ○	. . . Points of interest or places mentioned in the text.

20. The Last Part of the Dipsea Trail

HOW TO GET THERE

BY BUS: GGT #63 (Stinson Beach/ Bolinas) to Pan Toll on weekends and holidays

BY CAR: Highways 101, 1 and Panoramic to Pan Toll (see Chapter 19)

FEATURES

The Dipsea race began unofficially in 1904 when two San Francisco Olympic Club members ran 6.8 miles from Mill Valley over a ridge of Mt. Tamalpais to dip into the sea at Stinson Beach. The first official race took place in 1905, and since that year it has been an annual event in August. Nowadays the race attracts as many as 1500 runners—rather a crowd for some of the steep and narrow portions of the route. The best times have been just under 50 minutes for the rugged 6.8 miles.

Lazy hikers can enjoy the final, long, 3-mile-downhill stretch of the Dipsea Trail and its spectacular views without having to agonize through most of the corresponding uphill, by taking the bus back to their starting point. Some of the downhill is rather steep and rough, so unless you're very nimble or in training for the race, you will probably be more comfortable wearing hiking boots than sneakers.

DESCRIPTION

Head south from the ranger station on the paved road. Just past the sign for the Steep Ravine Trail on the right is a sign for the Old Mine Trail on the left. This trail parallels the road for ¼ mile and then rejoins it; you can choose either, but paths are more pleasant than paving. Both road and trail run under Douglas fir, bay and coast live oak to emerge on an open hillside. (Someplace around here there actually was a mine; apparently optimistic prospectors once sought gold, silver and other precious metals on this and other parts of the mountain.)

Beyond the rejoining of road and trail, you pass an unsigned trail going

As the Dipsea Trail descends toward Stinson Beach, you look out over the Seadrift sandspit and Bolinas Lagoon

The Dipsea Trail descends a grassy gully . . .

. . . and soon goes through the Steep Ravine redwoods

off to the right and descend toward the signpost visible less than 100 yards ahead. As you walk you can see the Tiburon peninsula, Angel Island, Mt. Diablo, Oakland, much of San Francisco, and Montara Mountain to the south. In the middle distance you can also see much of the Marin headlands and can recognize the ridges separated by Frank Valley, Green Gulch and Tennessee Valley. The tops of the Transamerica and Bank of America buildings peek coyly from behind the Vortac on its knoll.

Turn right, as per the sign *Dipsea Trail to Stinson Beach*, and walk toward the ocean. In summer the hills are platinum from the wild oats shimmering in sun and wind. An occasional stand of dark-green fir or gray rock outcropping provides contrast. The view of the hills, the Pacific, and the Farallon Islands is marred only by a line of utility poles. Soon you come to a trail that makes a short detour up a bank to a grove of trees on the right.

Here is Lone Tree Spring, constructed by the Tamalpais Conservation Club in 1917. The once lonely, large redwood tree in front of it now has the company of a number of its fellows, plus some bays and firs.

The road descends gradually, passes under the power lines and ascends a small knoll. From here, with binoculars, you can see some of the imaginative architecture on the Muir Beach headlands to the south. Continue on the road, or on the trail that has been running alongside and occasionally crossing it, until you pass under the power lines again. A blue-and-white sign indicates where the Dipsea Trail leaves the fire road here and veers right toward a forest. The trail skirts the trees briefly, then turns left to descend a steep, grassy stretch. At the bottom of it, whence you can see Bolinas mesa to the north, bear right toward the forest. The Dipsea Trail now descends through an area dense with bay trees, red elderberry bushes and some poison oak. A youth

Mushrooms spring up along the trail after a rain

conservation corps worked on this part of the trail in 1976, shoring up the sides with log berms and making steps with old railroad ties. Still, it's steep enough that most nonracers would prefer to take it at no faster than 2 miles per hour. At one point anyone more than 4 feet tall has to stoop to squeeze under a fallen bay that is still branching toward the sun—evidence of the tenacity with which these trees reach for light and cling to life. Now you can hear Webb Creek cascading on your right and see the Steep Ravine redwoods. Cross Webb Creek on a footbridge, turn

left and walk toward the dam visible 50 yards downstream.

At the dam turn right, uphill, and in 50 yards pass a fire road that leads left to Shoreline Highway. Continue toward Panoramic Highway, to a stile on the left bearing the sign *National Park Boundary*. The Dipsea Trail currently runs through this stile and over a hilly, thistly cow pasture. (The traditional Dipsea route from here to Stinson Beach was partly on the highway and partly on or bordering private property. For the greater convenience of racers, hikers, drivers and property owners, the park service has rerouted the trail.) You cross a dirt road, go through another stile, and continue over the barren hills, heading almost directly toward the Seadrift sandspit visible in the distance. As you descend toward the town of Stinson Beach, you get a good view of the steep cliffs that form its backdrop, and a glimpse of some of its imaginative hillside domestic architecture, including Valentino Agnoli's mushroom-shaped house.

The trail comes out at a stile on Panoramic Highway just above its junction with Shoreline Highway. From here it's a short walk north on Shoreline to the town, the beach, and the bus stop, which is marked by a sign at Shoreline and Calle del Mar. For suggestions on entertaining yourself in Stinson Beach, see Chapter 23.

21. Around Rock Springs

HOW TO GET THERE

BY BUS: GGT #63 (Stinson Beach/ Bolinas) to Pan Toll on weekends and holidays.

BY CAR: Take Highways 101, 1 and Panoramic to Pan Toll (see Ch. 19). Or continue on Southside Road for a mile to the free Rock Springs parking lot.

FEATURES

One of the features that make Mt. Tamalpais so picturesque is the occurrence of large patches of serpentine. This rock, a metamorphosed peridotite, was originally part of the deep-ocean floor. How did it get up on Mt. Tamalpais? This question baffled geologists until recently, when the new theory of plate tectonics suggested an answer. Serpentine is found only in highly disrupted zones, for example, in the Coast Ranges and the Sierra Nevada. It can be almost any color; most of it on Mt. Tamalpais is greenish.

Serpentine is the official California state rock. The state mineral is, of course, gold; and most Californians know that the state flower is the California poppy, the state tree the redwood, and the state animal the extinct California grizzly bear. But how many are aware that the state insect is the California dogface butterfly, or the state reptile the Mojave Desert tortoise? Armed with this knowledge, one might win a few barroom bets.

This hike provides some good views in clear weather, and it passes a number of good picnic spots.

Facilities: Restrooms at Rock Springs, Potrero Camp and Laurel Dell.

DESCRIPTION

From Pan Toll cross the highway and find the Old Mine Trail heading uphill from the left of the small maintenance building. The first ¾ mile of the Old

San Francisco viewed over a fog bank from the top of the Old Mine Trail

Serpentine outcropping near Rock Springs

Bay, madrone and tanbark oak trees near Rock Springs on the Bernstein Trail

Mine Trail is the only steep part of this hike. The reward for climbing it is an increasingly panoramic view of San Francisco's beach; Seal Rocks and the Cliff House are visible through binoculars, and to the west are the vast ocean and the Farallon Islands.

Signs indicate where the trail turns right, into a grove of Douglas fir, live oak, tanbark oak and bay; then it curves left to join the riding/hiking trail and continues uphill, providing views of the San Rafael—Richmond Bridge, the East Bay and Mt. Diablo. As you come over a rise and see the ocean far below, the trail curves right (sign) for the final uphill stretch, passing an outcropping of peridotitic rock on the right. From here you can clearly see all three of Mt. Tam's peaks.

Now the trail goes slightly downhill and runs through a striking jumble of gray-green serpentine. This rock has apparently been subjected to a lot of shearing and fracturing. Some of it is so shiny that it looks almost greasy. Just beyond the serpentine patch, at a Y (riding/hiking-trail sign), stay left and soon descend, crossing a paved road and the highway, to the Rock Springs parking lot. Go through a turnstile where a number of signs list water-district regulations.

For almost a century there was a little spring here under the trees, where hikers counted on filling their canteens. In the summer of 1972 it abruptly disappeared—bulldozed by the water district. The district has constructed a new spring not far away, on the Cataract

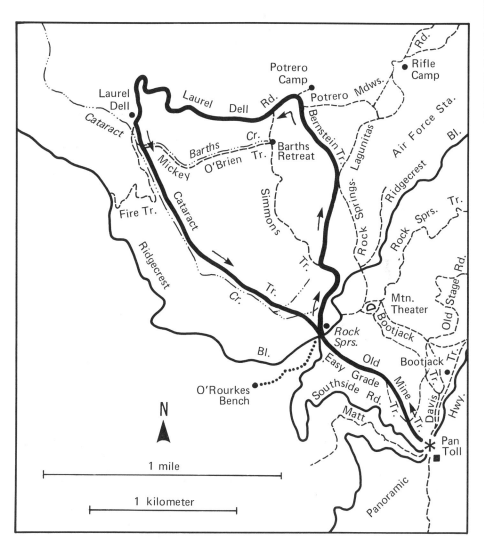

Potrero
Camp

Rifle
Camp

Laurel
Dell

Laurel Dell Rd.

Potrero Mdws.

Cataract

Barths Cr.

Barths
Retreat

Mickey O'Brien Tr.

Bernstein Tr.

Air Force Sta.

Bl.

Fire Tr.

Cataract

Simmons

Ridgecrest

Rock Springs-Lagunitas

Ridgecrest

Rock Sprs. Tr.

Cr.

Tr.

Tr.

Mtn.
Theater

Old Stage Rd.

Bl.

Rock
Sprs.

Bootjack

Bootjack Tr.

O'Rourkes
Bench

Easy Grade

Old Mine Tr.

Davis Tr.

Hwy.

Southside Rd.

Matt

Pan
Toll

N

Panoramic

1 mile

1 kilometer

Trail, but a sign on a nearby water tank states, *The water here does not meet public health standards,* and advises using the drinking fountain at the Mountain Theater.

A sign about 100 yards north of the turnstile (toward the power pole) indicates *Bernstein Trail to Potrero.* Take this trail, which leads uphill past another conspicuous outcropping of gray-green serpentine. Now bear left to enter a woods of Douglas fir, madrone, coast live oak and canyon live oak—the

LEGEND

*✱ ➘	. . . . Hiking Trail Routes
—①—	. . Car Access Road or Highway
••••••••	. . . . Side Trip
– – – –	. . . . . . Alternate Trail Routes
———	. . . . Park Boundaries
—·—·—	. . . . City Limits
〰〰	. . . . Creeks and Streams
≈≈≈	. . . . Shoreline
△ ■ ● ○	. . Points of interest or places mentioned in the text.

last identifiable by its lead-colored underleaves. A dead tree off to the right of the trail is a favorite haunt of busy, noisy woodpeckers. After a long half mile the Bernstein Trail joins the Rock Springs—Lagunitas Fire Road for 100 yards, and then verges off to the left at the signpost marked *Potrero* (the fire road continues to Rifle Camp). Take the trail, and soon reach the crest of the ridge. A few hundred feet over the crest, just before the trail curves north, a break in the dense manzanita to the left leads to a view point overlooking the Pacific Ocean and Farallon Islands.

The trail now descends through an unusual grove of giant chinquapins, recognizable by their yellow underleaves and the fallen burrs on the ground. Beyond the chinquapins a huge tanbark oak used to grow, but it was one of the casualties of the 1974 snowfall: it crashed down on the trail.

As you continue to descend, you find yourself in a grove of Sargent cypress—a sign that you are now walking over a serpentine area. Serpentine is deficient in some of the elements most plants need for growth, such as calcium, whereas it contains magnesium in amounts that are toxic for many plants. Therefore vegetation on it is limited in both variety and size. Some species, like this cypress, grow only on or near serpentine areas. Other species have a serpentine form that is stunted, compared with their form when growing in ordinary soil. The trail soon comes to a T in a serpentine-chaparral community. Three chaparral species grow only on serpentine: a manzanita (*Arctostaphylos montana*), the scrubby leather oak (*Quercus durata*) and a ceanothus (*C. Jepsonii*) with small hollylike leaves and, in the spring, purple flowers.

Picnic lunch at Potrero Camp

Turn right here (no sign) and descend to the Laurel Dell Fire Road. Go left on it for 50 feet to find the trail heading north to Potrero Camp (restrooms, picnic tables). Potrero Meadows extend to the northeast. This flat expanse was once occupied by Rocky Ridge, which slid down the mountain fairly recently, as geologic time goes— perhaps a few thousand years ago. A similar slide here today might fill man-made Bon Tempe and Alpine lakes, with disastrous effects on Marin's water supply.

Leave Potrero Camp by taking the Laurel Dell Fire Road west. Passing the road to Barths Retreat on the left, you come upon a vista that encompasses Alpine Lake, the Meadow Club golf course, Fairfax and its surrounding hills, and Mt. St. Helena to the north. Unfortunately, nowadays this vista generally encompasses a considerable amount of smog too. The road continues through a serpentine area and then enters a Douglas fir forest—a sign that you are back on normal soil, since fir won't grow on sepentine. A mile from Potrero Camp you reach Laurel Dell, an extensive picnic ground shaded by lofty oak, fir and bay trees. A substantial restroom building now dominates the site, providing a somewhat jarring note.

From Laurel Dell return to Rock Springs via the Cataract Trail, one of the most picturesque on Mt. Tamalpais. Just south of Laurel Dell this trail splits left from the fire road to cross Barths Creek. Now it follows Cataract Creek past waterfalls, ferns and moss-covered boulders. At one point a landslide on the right gives evidence, on a small

scale, of the kind of earth movements that have taken place on the mountain. The absence of signs, and the presence of numerous unmapped trails veering off to the left, may make the route appear somewhat confusing, but as long as you stay close to the creek you will end up at Rock Springs. From here you can return to Pan Toll via the Old Mine Trail or via the Mountain Theater and the Easy Grade Trail.

Variations: On a hot day the Mickey O'Brien or Barths Creek Trail provides a shady, cool route to Laurel Dell. This trail suffered severe snow damage in January 1974. It begins at the west side of Barths Retreat and runs above the south bank of Barths Creek through fir forest and patches of huckleberry. When you emerge from the trees in a short ¾ mile, turn right to reach Laurel Dell.

Another variation is to take the Simmons Trail, which runs between Rock Springs and Barths Retreat over a serpentine ridge where the demarcation of plant communities is strikingly evident. This is another trail that suffered severe snow damage.

SIDE TRIP

For more serpentine and more views of City and ocean, walk southwest from the Rock Springs parking lot across Ridgecrest and climb the knoll. Here is another large outcropping, greasy-looking in places. Continue southwest, to the right of the windswept trees, and in a short quarter mile come to O'Rourke's Bench, a memorial to "Dad" O'Rourke, one of the founders of the Mountain Theater. From this knoll you can look over to Bolinas, on the other side of the fault zone.

22. Muir Woods

HOW TO GET THERE

BY BUS: As this book goes to press, GGT is running buses (#61) to Muir Woods on weekends and holidays, and has started a ferry-bus route from San Francisco via Larkspur to the Woods. These services may vary seasonally, or may be discontinued, so check with GGT before starting out. See also *Alternate routes* at the end of this chapter.

BY CAR: From Highway 101 go west on Highway 1 at the Stinson Beach exit. After 3 winding miles, where Highway 1 continues to Stinson Beach turn right on Panoramic Highway; after 1 mile, turn left on Muir Woods Road (sign) and follow it 1 mile to the monument parking lot.

MAP: Trail map available at entrance gate

FEATURES

Hiking in a virgin redwood forest is an experience available only in northern California. A hundred and fifty million years ago, the ancestors of these giant trees were common throughout the Northern Hemisphere. Now two genera remain, in very small ranges: the coast redwood *(Sequoia sempervirens)* in the fog belt along the northern California coast, and the giant sequoia *(Sequoiadendron giganteum)* on the western slope of the Sierra. The tallest trees in the world are the coast redwoods that grow about 300 miles north of the Bay Area (some of them in controversial Redwood National Park); the biggest

Iris in the redwood forest

Wedding party in the Muir Woods parking lot

are the giant sequoias that grow more than 100 miles southeast. (The oldest trees in the world are not redwoods, but the bristlecone pines in the White Mountains of California, near the Nevada border.) Although the trees of Muir Woods may not be the tallest or biggest or oldest in the world, they are, by virtue of their situation near a great metropolitan tourist center, the most visited.

Muir Woods is an inspiring example of what one dedicated conservationist can do to preserve a beautiful area for following generations. This canyon full of redwoods would undoubtedly have been logged or flooded for a reservoir in the first decade of the 20th century except for one strong-minded man, William Kent. In 1905 Kent purchased 300 acres of the canyon for $45,000, intending to save it for the public, and three years later he per-

Lining up at the entrance gate to Muir Woods

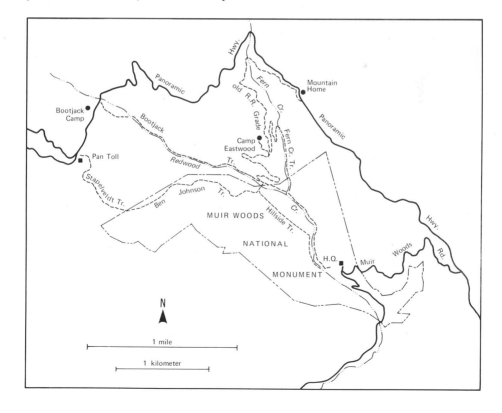

suaded President Theodore Roosevelt to make it a national monument named for John Muir.

Nowadays Muir Woods is one of the pre-eminent tourist attractions in the Bay Area: on any day, and especially on weekends, charter buses unload hundreds of travelers from every part of the world, wearing costumes that range from saris to levis and conversing in a Babel of tongues—but usually quietly. The awe-inspiring qualities of the forest seem to have a subduing effect on even the most ebullient visitor.

If you are a Bay Arean entertaining friends or relatives from out of town or out of country, you are almost obligated to take them to Muir Woods for an hour or so. Even the very young and the very old can enjoy the level trails on either side of Redwood Creek within a mile of the visitor center.

Facilities: Parking just outside the gate; water, restrooms, phone, snack shop, book shop and gift shop.

Regulations: Open 8 a.m. to sunset; $.50 entrance fee for each person between the ages of 16 and 65. No dogs on trails; no picnicking; no camping.

Phone: 388-2595

DESCRIPTION

From the parking lot walk north to the visitor center. Along the way, markers point out common plants of the redwood ecosystem. Some of the markers are duplicated in braille so that the blind can read them. Near the visitor center is a cross-section of a redwood, whose rings are labeled with various historical events.

Now walk across the rustic bridge to the west side of Redwood Creek, the stream that flows through the monument. If you're here in winter, you may see salmon and steelhead fighting their way upstream to spawn. Walking north along the creek, you soon come to Bohemian Grove, where members of San Francisco's elite Bohemian Club encamped in 1892. They were considering buying land here for a permanent camp, but found the place too cold and clammy, and decided on their present location near the Russian River instead.

At Bohemian Grove begins a ¼-mile nature trail. An unusually attractive leaflet describing the trail is available from boxes at either end. (Deposit $.25 in one of the boxes if you decide to keep it.) In 1976 this was designated a

Pick the blackberries if you want to, but WATCH OUT FOR THE POISON OAK!

Redwood sorrel, or oxalis, abounds on the floor of Muir Woods

Among the giant trees on the well-traveled valley floor of Muir Woods

National Recreation Trail and a tree along it, judged to be about 200 years old, was christened the Bicentennial Tree.

Follow the nature trail to its end, near another footbridge. Cross this bridge to return to the east side of Redwood Creek and Cathedral Grove, which contains what is perhaps the most poignant memorial plaque in the monument:

"Here in this grove of enduring Redwoods, preserved for posterity, members of the United Nations Conference on International Organization met on May 19, 1945,

to honor the memory of Franklin Delano Roosevelt, thirty-first President of the United States, Chief Architect of the United Nations and Apostle of Peace for all Mankind."

Ironic as this inscription may seem from the perspective of the 1970s, one cannot help being moved by the sight of continual visitors from various members of the United Nations solemnly studying it.

Walk north along the east bank of the creek another ¼ mile to reach the William Kent Memorial Tree, a 273-foot Douglas fir, the tallest tree in the monument. The plaque honoring Kent

Resting by Redwood Creek in Muir Woods

is set in a 3½-ton boulder, which hikers from the Tamalpais Conservation Club brought down the mountain on the railroad and rolled by hand to its present site.

Turn back to Cathedral Grove and continue south on the east side of the creek. Soon you pass the memorial to Gifford Pinchot, Theodore Roosevelt's Chief Forester and one of the giants of the early-20th-century conservation movement. You can end this walk with a cup of coffee at the visitor center, where your friends from out of town can purchase postcards to send the folks back home.

ALTERNATE ROUTES

The parking lot at Muir Woods on sunny weekends frequently resembles the one at the Marina Safeway or the Shattuck Avenue Berkeley Co-op on Saturday afternoon—an endless stream of cars circling steadily around at a speed of ½ mile per hour while they wait for someone to pull out. You can avoid this scene by taking the GGT bus when it is running to the Woods.

Unless you are escorting people who are very young, very old or very infirm, when both the #61 and #63 buses are running you can take a downhill route to the forest floor from one of the trailheads on Panoramic Highway. Such a trip will be much less crowded and much more scenic than starting in the midst of the tourists. For example:

From Mountain Home take the Old Railroad Grade and Fern Canyon Trail.

From Bootjack take the Bootjack Trail.

From Pan Toll take the Stapleveldt and Ben Johnson trails.

All these routes are shown on the Mt. Tamalpais State Park map and on the Erickson map of Tamalpais trails.

23. Stinson Beach

HOW TO GET THERE

BY BUS: GGT #63 (Stinson Beach/ Bolinas) on weekends and holidays. The inhabitants of this traffic-clogged town—like those of Sausalito—will be grateful to you for coming by bus.

BY CAR: From Highway 101 go west on Highway 1 at the Stinson Beach exit and continue following signs for Stinson Beach, which is 23 miles north of San Francisco. You can return the same way, or by Muir Woods Road, or by Panoramic Highway. All these routes are extremely scenic and extremely narrow and winding.

FEATURES

Stinson Beach (originally called Willow Camp) has been a seaside resort for over a century. In the 1870s Captain Alfred Easkoot rented out tents on the beach. During the '80s, Nathan Stinson opened his own resort in competition with Easkoot. Around the turn of the century several businessmen seriously considered building a railroad over the mountain from Mill Valley down Steep Ravine to Stinson Beach and Bolinas. Among them was William Kent, who prudently bought up much of the Bolinas Lagoon sandspit, as well as Steep Ravine. If the railroad plan had succeeded, Stinson Beach and Bolinas might have become grand, fashionable resorts like those on the East Coast and in Southern California. Kent, in his later days as a great conservationist, was probably just as glad that the plan fell through. The sandspit, christened Seadrift by the Kent family, is still a private development adjoining the park. The GGNRA took the rest of the beach over from the state-park system in 1977.

Facilities: Restrooms, picnic tables,

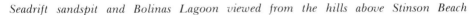

Seadrift sandspit and Bolinas Lagoon viewed from the hills above Stinson Beach

grills, phone; ordinarily Stinson has water fountains and cold showers, but don't count on them during periods of drought. Snack bar during summer. Swimming is popular here, but signs warn that you swim at your own risk because no lifeguards are on duty. Surf fishing is possible.

Regulations: Hours: 9 a.m.-6 p.m. in winter, 9 a.m.-10 p.m. in summer; no pets; no camping.

DESCRIPTION

The main automobile entrance to the beach's huge parking lot is clearly marked by a sign on Highway 1. Stinson's broad, white strand is suitable for just about any beach activity—Frisbee, volleyball and football as well as sunbathing and swimming. This beach's popularity is due partly to its sheltered position: both Bolinas headland and Point Reyes protect it to some degree from rough ocean currents and cold northwest winds. However, *no* ocean swimming in northern California is comfortably warm or truly safe, so don't expect Laguna Beach.

If you want to get away from the crowds, you can stroll along the nearly

Clamming on Stinson Beach in December when the crowds are gone

three miles of sand. To the southeast the strand ends at Mickey's Beach, where students of rock-climbing practice their skills. To the northwest is the sandspit housing exclusive Seadrift. This sandspit has been the subject of litigation off and on for over three quarters of a century. After William Kent purchased it in the early 1900s, squatters denied his claim and pitched

To avoid the crowds, visit Stinson Beach in winter

Rock fishing south of Stinson Beach

Climbers' Rock at Mickey's Beach, on the south end of Stinson Beach

tents on it. The descendants of the 1846 Mexican grantee claimed *they* had title to it, and so did Nathan Stinson. These challenges were eventually quashed, but Kent in about 1914 declared, "had it not been for the flood of litigation . . . we should have had a railroad into Bolinas more than ten years ago . . ." (quoted in Jack Mason's *Last Stage for Bolinas*). As you walk along the white sand you may be grateful to the squatters and other litigants.

In more recent years, controversy has centered over public access to Seadrift. The only road into the development is barred by a locked and guarded gate. For several years an iron fence ran across the beach into the ocean in an attempt to seal off Seadrift from hoi polloi. While the questions simmers in the courts and the North Central Coast Regional Commission, in practice the high-tide line is the effective boundary. (If you're walking on wet sand, you're probably not trespassing.)

If you get tired of the beach, the village offers other ways of passing the time. It contains some bars and restaurants, a health-food delicatessen and a cozy bookstore.

BOLINAS RIDGE

Chapters 24 through 26

Historians of early Marin claim that the redwoods on Bolinas Ridge were the equal of those in the Calaveras forest, some of them being 50 feet in circumference.

These big trees could hardly withstand Gold Rush San Francisco's insatiable demand for lumber. In 1849 hordes of lumberjacks poured in to what had been sleepy Rancho Baulines, and the original Mexican grantees soon found themselves virtually dispossessed. The history of this land grant is even more confused and litigious than that of most in Marin County—which is saying a good deal. As in so many of these cases, most of the property eventually ended up in the hands of Yankee lawyers.

During the 1850's, when the sawmills were running full blast, saloons and gambling parlors flourished at Bolinas

The south end of Bolinas Ridge Trail begins in a park-like forest of Douglas fir

and at Dogtown, two miles north.

Marin historian Jack Mason quotes one of the lumberjacks, Charles Lauff (the same fellow that went bear-hunting with William A. Richardson on Christmas of 1847—see Ch. 17) as follows: "I will never forget my first Sunday. Everyone observed the Sabbath, feasting and carousing. There was a small saloon at Dogtown. The whiskey would kill at 30 yards, and it was all off with the poor devil who took an overdose. On my first Sunday I witnessed a barbecue, joined in by everybody. It happened to be deer meat, and there was plenty of it. (The town got its name from vagrant dogs used in hunting deer and bear.). . .At night a large bonfire roared and the population—the sober ones—sang songs until the wee hours."

Yerba santa blooms among the chaparral on Bolinas Ridge

Vultures wheel above the ridge

In 1868 the citizens of Dogtown, hoping to attract marriageable women, officially changed its name to Woodville. This name still appears on the topo, although virtually all of the town itself has vanished.

When you walk along Bolinas Ridge today, you would never guess its raucous past. It is, in fact, the most tranquil, lonely part of the GGNRA. Even on a fair weekend you can walk for miles along the ridge trail and encounter only a few equestrians and fewer hikers. On a weekday you may not encounter anyone, except perhaps a black-tailed deer or two.

At present, no buses run very close to Bolinas Ridge—which may help to explain why there are so few hikers on it! However, experienced, vigorous hikers can utilize the Erickson map, the topo maps and the GGT weekend bus schedule to travel the whole ridge in one day. To do this, take the early morning #64 (Inverness) bus to Shafter Bridge, Samuel P. Taylor State Park or the trailhead a mile east of Olema—all of which are described in the last chapter of this book. (Taylor Park is a regular stop; if you want to get off at either of the others, confer with the driver. Note that there are *two* trailheads at Shafter Bridge, one on either side of the creek: the eastern one leads to Kent Lake, the western one to Bolinas Ridge.) Hike south along the Bolinas Ridge Trail, and descend to pick up the #63 southbound bus at the junction of Highway 1 and the Olema-Bolinas Road, or at Audubon Canyon Ranch, or at Stinson Beach, or at Pan Toll. As these routes range in length from about 10 miles to 18 miles, don't try it unless you're sure you can finish—and BE CERTAIN you have an up-to-date bus schedule. As this book goes to press, the early #64 arrives at Samuel P. Taylor Park at 9:42 and the latest #63 leaves Bolinas at 5:32, allowing almost 8 hours for hiking. (You can, of course, arrange a two-car shuttle from one of these points to another.)

Regulations: No trailbikes, no motorized vehicles; no smoking on trails; no guns.

MAPS: Topos *Bolinas, San Geronimo* and *Inverness;* C.E. Erickson's *Recreational Map: Golden Gate National Recreation Area;* USGS *Point Reyes National Seashore and Vicinity.*

Equestrians on the Bolinas Ridge Trail above Olema Valley as fog lifts above Inverness Ridge in background

24. The Southern Part of Bolinas Ridge

HOW TO GET THERE

BY BUS: See the Introduction to Bolinas Ridge

BY CAR: Proceed to Rock Springs as per Ch. 21; from there drive north on Ridgecrest Blvd. 3 miles to its junction with the Fairfax-Bolinas Road and park on the roadside. The Fairfax-Bolinas Road too is a possible access route WHEN IT'S OPEN: it is shut down during extremely wet weather because of landslide hazard and during extremely dry weather because of fire hazard. Following the route of an old stage road, it is highly (literally) scenic but also narrow and winding—not recommended for people who get carsick.

FEATURES

Even though lumbering continued around here until fairly recently, much of the ridge itself is crowned with tall redwoods and Douglas firs that provide an almost park-like ambience. From time to time as you walk along the fairly level trail, clearings offer breathtaking views over Bolinas Lagoon and the ocean. And on a foggy or misty day, this is an especially fascinating, mysterious place to hike.

You can walk as long as you want, and then turn back—but please don't plan to make a loop return via the trail that the Erickson map shows running parallel to the ridge trail about ¼ mile west of it. This trail is at present nonexistent, or at least unfindable.

Facilities: None; surface water unsafe, carry water.

Regulations: No camping, no fires. (This is a great place to bring a horse, but a terrible place to bring a dog: he will want to get off leash, and if he

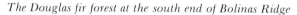

The Douglas fir forest at the south end of Bolinas Ridge

does, he will want to chase wildlife.) Ridgecrest Blvd. closed ½ hour after sundown to ½ hour before sunrise.

DESCRIPTION

Find the sign for the Bolinas Ridge Trail leading north from the road junction (not from a few hundred feet down the Fairfax-Bolinas Road, as Erickson shows it). The sign gives the distance to Samuel P. Taylor Park as 11.4, and although it doesn't so specify, these are miles, not kilometers! The trail begins in a beautiful forest of redwood, Douglas fir and tanbark oak, with an understory of ceanothus, huckleberry and ferns. You soon pass the unsigned Bourne Trail leading down to Audubon Canyon Ranch. (This trail appears on the topo map but not on the Erickson map.) When there's a break in the forest, you can see Bolinas lagoon, town and mesa far below. You are actually looking across the San Andreas fault zone, which runs under the lagoon.

Soon the forest gives way to a more chaparral-like growth, including scrub oak, manzanita and occasional chinquapin. From time to time you pass the distinctive yellow-topped stakes that show this route is part of the California Riding and Hiking Trail system—a project of the 1940s that was never quite completed. On your right is a steep gulch full of charred tree trunks from the fire of 1945. As the trail ascends slightly, you can look east to see Mt. Tamalpais, part of the Bay and Mt. Diablo; to the north is Pine Mountain Ridge and, in clear weather, Mt. St. Helena in the distance.

At a power line you pass a sign for *Pikes Ridge*. Soon the trail goes back into redwoods and tanbark oak. In spring, iris and yellow violets grace the forest floor. Amid the attractive ferns and salal is, unfortunately, some of that hardy European interloper, broom.

California Riding and Hiking Trail sign on Bolinas Ridge

Milkmaids—one of the earliest spring flowers

Occasional trails run off to the left, one of them leading to a horse trough. In a gully on the left slope there was once a copper mine, which is still shown on the maps. On the whole this mine was not a success, although one company did extract 22,500 pounds from it during World War I. At the

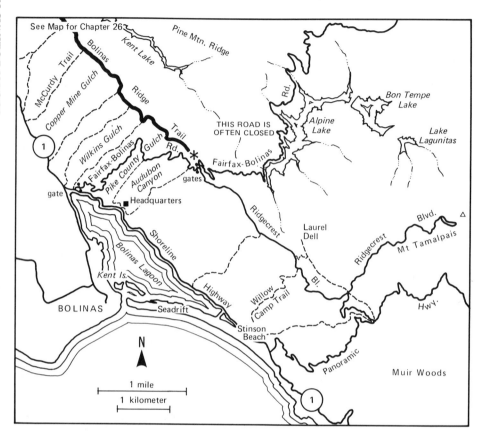

bottom of the slope to your right is Kent Lake—but you can't see it from here.

After 3.4 miles of hiking you reach the sign for the McCurdy Trail, which leads down to Woodville. This junction is a good destination for a leisurely afternoon's hike, but if you want to, you can continue farther along the mostly level trail. In a couple of miles it will come out of the forest and offer a view over pastoral Olema Valley.

LEGEND

✱ ➤	. . . . Hiking Trail Routes
—①—	. . Car Access Road or Highway
••••••••	. . . . Side Trip
– – – – –	. . . . . Alternate Trail Routes
————	. . . . Park Boundaries
—·—·—	. . . . City Limits
～～～～	. . . . Creeks and Streams
≋≋≋	. . . . Shoreline
△ ■ ● ○	. . . Points of interest or places mentioned in the text.

25. Audubon Canyon Ranch

HOW TO GET THERE

BY BUS: GGT #63 (Bolinas) on weekends and holidays; for Marin County service, phone 453-2100.

BY CAR: From Highway 101 take narrow, winding Highway 1 west to Stinson Beach and continue northwest for 3½ miles.

MAPS: Trail map available at headquarters

FEATURES

Audubon Canyon Ranch is an enclave on the slope of Bolinas Ridge, surrounded by GGNRA.

Even people who ordinarily consider ornithology a bore—or who don't know what it is—are fascinated by the sight of egrets and great blue herons feeding their young in the treetop nests of Audubon Canyon. This unique sanctuary offers the big birds a protected nesting site in a redwood grove, near an ample source of food in Bolinas Lagoon.

Looking down into Audubon Canyon from Henderson Overlook . . .

The continued existence of the rookery is something of a miracle, because beleaguered conservationists have had to defend it during the last few years against threats of logging, subdividing, highway widening and marina building, and against the great oil spill of 1971. Somehow a dedicated group of volunteers, with the Marin Audubon Society as its nucleus, managed to raise enough money to purchase not only Audubon Canyon itself, but adjoining Volunteer Canyon (named for the workers who kept the oil out of Bolinas Lagoon) and Kent Island in the lagoon.

In 1975 disaster struck the egrets when raccoons predated many of their nests. Before the raccoons could be captured and released in other parts of the county, they had dispatched most of the egret eggs and chicks. In 1977 the staff at the ranch became seriously

. . . to see egrets and herons nesting

Starting up the trail to the overlook from the Audubon Canyon Ranch headquarters

concerned when the egrets did not show up at their normal time. Eventually, by six weeks after the usual time, 47 pair of egrets had arrived and started nests. No one knows whether their delay was due to the previous predation, two years of drought, or something else.

Audubon Canyon is an excellent place to bring children, as well as visitors to the Bay Area, who probably have never seen anything like it. The most interesting time to visit the ranch is during May and early June, when the nestlings have hatched and are squawking for food. If you don't want to take the 4-mile hike suggested below, you can content yourself with a short walk to the bird overlook and perhaps a stroll around the nature trail.

Don't forget to bring binoculars, opera glasses, telescopes or any other equipment that might be used for bird-watching.

Facilities: Parking, water, restrooms, picnic tables, museum, bookstore.

Regulations: Open 10 a.m.-4 p.m. weekends and holidays from March 1 through July 4; open to schools and other groups by appointment Tuesday through Friday. Free, but donations welcome. Pets not allowed.

Phone: 383-1644

DESCRIPTION

Begin by registering at headquarters, a handsome old ranch house that dates from 1875. Pick up a trail map and whatever other literature the volunteers are handing out. Next, you can go back to the big former barn that houses the bookstore and museum; or you can postpone this until after you've seen the birds.

The main trail to the bird overlook begins just north of the ranch house. It soon makes a U at the Clem Miller Overlook, named for the late Congressman who worked so hard to establish Point Reyes National Seashore. You can rest on a bench here and observe herons, egrets and other birds fishing in Bolinas Lagoon.

Now climb a steep but short half mile to the side trail that goes right to the Henderson Overlook, where informal wood seating has been installed for watching the birds.

Here you are slightly above the nests, which are in the tops of second-growth redwoods. The grove is a scene of constant activity as the parents fly to and from the lagoon to fetch food for their demanding nestlings. The graceful flight of the adults is in sharp contrast to the raucous, undignified behavior of their young. The keen observer will note that both egrets and herons practice sexual equality: males and females of each species bear the same plumage, incubate the eggs and feed the young.

When you can tear yourself away from the birds, continue up the fairly steep trail, under the shade of bay, oak and buckeye. In spring the path is bordered by blooming yerba santa, woolly sunflower, hedge nettle, pitcher sage, nightshade and sticky monkeyflower.

After about a mile of ascent the trail levels off under redwoods and begins to descend toward the head of the canyon. here a creek splashes down past ferns, aralia and horsetail, and a rustic bench invites the hiker to rest.

The trail continues by contouring along the south side of the canyon, under redwoods and bays. You may find some columbine here. In ½ mile you emerge from the forest and after a brief ascent through chaparral overlook Bolinas Lagoon. Soon the Bourne

The trail winds up Audubon Canyon among redwoods

The morning glory is found throughout Marin County

The egret and heron feeding grounds in the mudflats of Bolinas Lagoon viewed from the hills above Audubon Canyon Ranch

Trail comes in from the left. From here on your route is all downhill and in the open, with views of Stinson Beach, Bolinas, and, in the distance, the Point Reyes peninsula. As you descend the grassy hillside you may see and hear finches, sparrows, blackbirds, hawks and quail; over 90 species of landbirds have been identified on the ranch, of which sixty are permanent residents.

The trail curves around under coast live oaks to return to the ranch buildings. Now you may wish to visit or revisit the museum and bookstore or to take one of the side trips mentioned below.

SIDE TRIPS

1-The Bert C. Harwell Nature Trail, which makes a 4/5 mile loop in the canyon just north of the ranch, is worth a visit, especially for children. Ask the volunteers at headquarters for a leaflet and map to accompany this walk.

2-When the tide is low you can explore Agate Beach, located 1½ miles west of central Bolinas, at the end of Elm Road. South of the beach is Duxbury Reef, named for a ship that ran aground on it in 1849. This reef is one of the best spots in the Bay Area for tidepooling. Until a few years ago, mussel fanciers used to swarm over the rocks during minus tides to gather the makings for Moules a la Mariniere. Finally, overcollecting— by students as well as cooks—began to threaten the reef's ecosystem, and the county put the area under its protection. Now visitors may study marine life here but may not remove any of it.

26. Samuel P. Taylor State Park and the Northern Part of Bolinas Ridge

HOW TO GET THERE

BY BUS: GGT #64 (Inverness) on weekends and holidays

BY CAR: From Highway 101 take Sir Francis Drake Blvd. 14 miles west to Lagunitas and thence about 2 miles farther to the main park entrance.

MAPS: Trail map of Taylor Park available from headquarters

FEATURES

Samuel P. Taylor State Park is one of the very few car-camping areas near both the GGNRA and Point Reyes National Seashore, and therefore it is immensely popular. It is named for a forty-niner from New York State who made his stake in the gold rush and subsequently purchased 100 acres on Lagunitas Creek, where in 1856 he established the first paper mill west of the Mississippi. It produced most of the newsprint for San Francisco's newspapers and much of the paper used for official documents in Sacramento. As the mill flourished, the settlement of Taylorville grew up around it, and after the North Pacific Coast Railroad came through Taylor's property in 1875 the area became a popular resort. It contained a campground and a three-story hotel, which occupied the site of the present picnic ground—rather hard to visualize today!

Taylor made the mistake of selling his riparian rights for $10,000, and the resulting diversion of water from the stream worked a hardship on the mill. Taylor died in 1886, the mill was foreclosed after the panic of 1893, and in 1915 the whole settlement burned down. The Marin Conservation League acquired the property in 1945, and subsequently turned it over to the state. The present park of nearly 2600 acres contains remarkably varied terrain: second-growth redwood groves along the creek, and open hills on the north side of Drake Blvd.

The route outlined here begins with 2 easy, level miles along the old railroad

Camping in the redwoods at Samuel P. Taylor State Park

A piece of the foundation of S.P. Taylor's paper mill still stands

grade to the most historic sections of the park. From here, energetic hikers can take off on a scenic climb up Bolinas Ridge. The loop trip described here is about 11 miles long, and involves fording Lagunitas Creek, which is easy enough at low water but might be considerably more difficult during or just after a rainy season. There is no drinkable water along most of the route.

Really vigorous hikers can travel the first half of the loop and continue south as described in the Introduction to Bolinas Ridge.

Facilities: Over a hundred picnic sites; 65 campsites with grills (no electrical outlets). Ordinarily these campsites are reservable through Ticketron, but during periods of drought, park facilities are on a first-come, first-served basis. The park also has camping facilities for backpackers and bicyclists. When the creek is high enough, fishing and swimming are possible.

Regulations: The standard state-park rules:

Pets must be on leash or housed at the campsite or in a vehicle; dogs over 5 months old must have license or other proof of current rabies inoculation; *no dogs on trails;* fee of $1 per dog per night.

No firearms.

Fires are allowed only in designated places, and you must bring your own fuel or buy it from the rangers; collecting wood is not allowed.

Overnight camping fees are $4 per night; day-use fee $1.50.

Phone: Taylor Park, 488-9897

LEGEND

✳ ⤳	. . . . Hiking Trail Routes
—①—	. . Car Access Road or Highway
• • • • • • • • •	. . . . Side Trip
— — — —	. . . . Alternate Trail Routes
— — —	. . . . Park Boundaries
— — —·—	. . . . City Limits
＼···＼	. . . . Creeks and Streams
≋	. . . . Shoreline
△ ■ • ○	. . . Points of interest or places mentioned in the text.

Often the hiker on Bolinas Ridge will have no company except deer and vultures

DESCRIPTION

Pick up the trail map from head-quarters as you enter. If you drove, park at the west end of the picnic ground (unless you are camping here). Walk north along the paved road to the campground. Just past campsite 13 find the trail running along the creek under redwood, bay, tanbark oak and occasional cottonwood trees. This creek is called Paper Mill in the park handouts, Lagunitas on the topo map. If you are walking here during a wet winter, you may see steelhead trout and salmon swimming upstream to spawn;

in spring you may see the resulting fingerlings.

The trail joins the road briefly and then runs along the creek again. You can follow either road or trail past the old dam site and a corral to reach the old mill site, a mile from the trailhead, where a plaque relates some of the mill's history. A few remnants of both the dam and the mill structures remain.

You can turn back here and take the Ox Trail that runs along the western side of the road to the trailhead; or you can continue walking west along the park maintenance road, almost im-

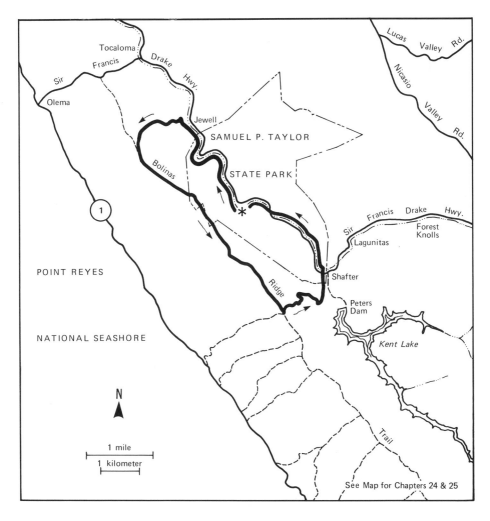

See Map for Chapters 24 & 25

The south Bolinas Ridge Trail is punctuated with stiles for hikers

mediately passing the bridge over the swimming hole on your right.

Your route curves north here. What you are walking on is actually the old roadbed for the narrow-gauge North Pacific Coast Railroad. The first train on this line ran from Sausalito to Tomales in 1875; subsequently track extended up to the Russian River and east as far as Cazadero. Over a thousand Chinese laborers were hired, at $1 per day, to build this railroad. Many of them had taken part a few years earlier in building the transcontinental railroad across the Sierra. The North Pacific Coast Railroad had a checkered financial career, and was eventually taken over by larger railroad companies. The completion of Sir Francis Drake Blvd. in 1930 finally drove the old narrow-gauge line out of business.

The old railroad grade soon reaches a fence marking the boundary between the state park and the GGNRA. Continue on the roadbed, under maple, buckeye and bay trees. Just across the creek you can glimpse the houses of the

village of Jewell, and hear the cars on the boulevard. Now a fire road goes uphill to your left; its gate bears a sign warning away motorized vehicles, but it opens for hikers. Be sure to close this and all subsequent gates behind you, because the park service leases the land to ranchers for cattle grazing. You will, in fact, undoubtedly encounter cows along much of the route. They are not unfriendly, but their fixed stare as you approach them can be somewhat unnerving, especially to a solitary hiker.

The road climbs gradually up through the remains of an old ranch. To the north is Black Mountain, to the east Barnabe Mountain (named for John C. Fremont's mule, who spent his last days as a pet of Samuel P. Taylor and is buried somewhere in the park). To the west is forested Inverness Ridge, part of Point Reyes National Seashore, with Mt. Wittenberg (1407') its high point.

After climbing less than a mile from the fire gate, you reach the hiking trail coming uphill from Sir Francis Drake Blvd. a mile east of Olema. As you continue to ascend gradually, narrow Tomales Bay extends its gleaming length to the northwest, and at its foot is Point Reyes Station. The trail levels out for a while, passing a corral, and then begins its steady climb again. You look out over the lush Olema Valley—and also over the San Andreas fault zone, which runs under Tomales Bay, the Olema Valley and Bolinas Lagoon. It was, in fact, in the Olema area that maximum displacement occurred during the 1906 earthquake—as much as 20 feet. Inverness Ridge, on the other side of the valley, is part of the Pacific Plate and is moving north at roughly 2 inches per year.

As the trail continues ever upward, from time to time passing through a ≻-shaped stile, the terrain and vegetation become wilder. Clumps of coyote brush grow on the grazing land and

Old Douglas firs on the trail to Shafter Bridge

Cattle grazing near the south Bolinas Ridge Trail warily eye approaching hikers

thick Douglas fir crown the nearby ridgetops. Under your feet in spring are wildflowers: poppies, buttercups, suncups, blue-eyed grass, and that common immigrant from the Old World, filaree. The trail passes directly under some large eucalyptus trees (not a bad spot for lunch), goes through yet another stile, and soon reaches a signed junction from where the trail to Shafter Bridge goes 1.9 miles downhill while the Bolinas Ridge Trail continues south along the spine of the ridge.

Unless you want to stay on the ridge, turn onto the Shafter Bridge trail. It almost immediately enters the forest and descends steadily through Douglas-fir, coast live oak, bay trees and a few California nutmegs (conifers with very sharp needles). Farther down, in the moister ground toward the bottom of the canyon, are redwood, alder and maple. The trail levels off along a tributary to Lagunitas Creek and shortly arrives at Shafter Bridge. (On the east side of the bridge is the fire road leading to Peters Dam and Kent Lake.) Now you have to scramble down the

bank and pick your way across Lagunitas Creek, avoiding the private property east of the park boundary. As noted above, this feat presents no difficulties at low water. Once across, head uphill on the north bank on an unsigned path that leads to the old railroad grade. It follows Lagunitas Creek downstream, running 50-100 feet above it under shady maples and redwoods. In the dense redwood forest along the creek some stumps remain from the period of lumbering. You pass the trail to Barnabe Mountain going off at an acute angle on your right. In spring, the right bank is bright with flowers, especially scarlet larkspur.

When you arrive at the Irving picnic area, the old railroad grade disappears. (Actually, it crosses the creek a few hundred feet to the west; you can still see the remains of its concrete bridge.) Take the riding-hiking trail that runs just above Sir Francis Drake Blvd., cross Barnabe Creek, and just before reaching the Madrone picnic area, descend to cross the highway and return to park headquarters.

INDEX